RAMBLINGS

IN
SUFFOLK'S LANDSCAPES

SHIONA HARDIE

Illustrations by JANICE MURRAY

Maps by HALLY HARDIE

SANDSCAPE

Published by:
Sandscape Publishing
18 Tennyson Close, Woodbridge, Suffolk IP12 4LB

ISBN 0 9526087 1 5

British Library Cataloguing in Publication Data:
a catalogue record for this book is available from the British Library.

The rights of way described in the book were correct, to the best of the author's
knowledge, at the time of writing. Neither the author nor the Publisher can accept
responsibility for damage, trespass or nuisance caused by others in the course of
negotiating the walks herein described or for errors due to the re-routeing or clos-
ing of footpaths, or misunderstood directions.

By the same author
Rambling in the Sandlings

Design & production:
Dick Richardson, Country Books, Little Longstone, Derbyshire DE45 1NN
Printed in England by:
MFP Design & Print, Stretford, Manchester M30 0JT
Cover origination by:
GA Graphics, Stamford, Lincolnshire PE9 2RB

"You can't judge Suffolk from a motor car, because the main roads happen to have the dullest landscape in the county."

Julian Tennyson, *"Suffolk Scene"*

ACKNOWLEDGEMENTS

Thanks must go to those without whom this book really would not have been possible – those who accompanied me through mud, crops, rain and shine. Helen with some personal history of undiscovered corners; Colin, in practice for the Himalayas; Janice who always brought the rain along; Bruce who plodded on in spite of the mud and the valiant Glennie whose four short legs never stopped. Thanks also to the several very helpful Rights of Way Officers of the County Council and to everyone I badgered for information. A particular thank you must go to Brian McColgan for the unenviable task of copy editing the original typescript and having to go through it all again in proof reading.

The map of Felsham Hall Farm was drawn from the map made by Wm. Warren in 1729. By permission of the Suffolk Record Office, Ipswich.

(*N*aps' *L*egen*ö*:

Dual Carriageway	Lake/Pond, River/Stream
'A' or 'B' Roads	
'C' or lesser roads	
Vehicular Tracks	Wood/Plantation
Footpaths or Bridleways	
Advised) Primary	Named Building
Routes) Secondary	Car Parking
Points of Interest, see text	Windmill
Embankment, Mound	

Scales vary from map to map, but are shown on each map. Each map has North at the top.

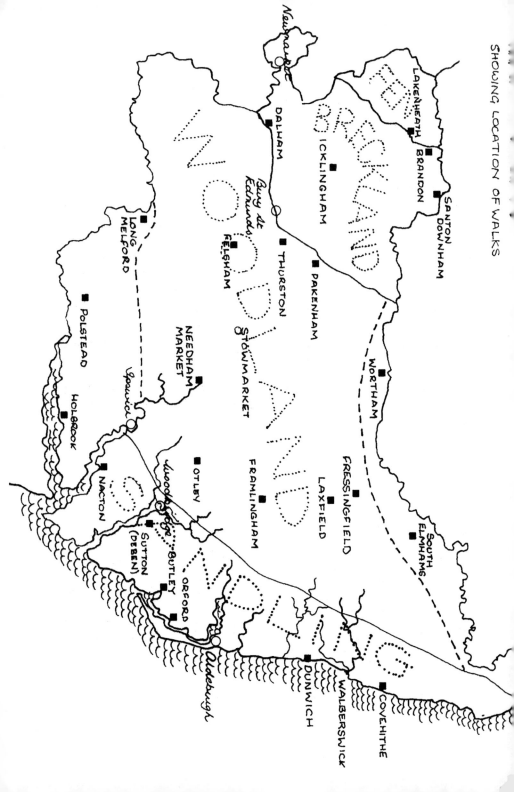

SHOWING LOCATION OF WALKS

C ONTENTS

INTRODUCTION

This is a walks book with a difference. The walks have all been planned with the aim of both helping the walker discover the rich variety of landscape within the county and gain a greater understanding of why it is as it is; how it was in times gone by and the impact of continual change brought about by human activity.

The initial chapters give a brief picture of the development of the Suffolk countryside from prehistoric times to the present and typical landscape features are looked at in some detail.

Walks. For convenience the walks are grouped loosely around the three regions of the county — Breckland, Woodland and Sandling. Each section has an introductory chapter on the landscape history and development of the area including its natural history. The woodland section contains more walks than the other two combined but it does cover two thirds of the county and includes a number of distinctive areas such as the Stour valley, the Waveney/Little Ouse valleys and the Shotley peninsula.

Each walk is accompanied by a sketch map and information on how to reach it, where to eat and any places of particular interest on the route or nearby. Walks vary in length from about 20km (13 miles) to 8km (5 miles) with suggestions for short cuts or extensions.

Routes. We have tried to find attractive circular routes but bear in mind that footpaths were originally made by people going about their daily business, travelling to and from work, from farm to field and between settlements, not for the convenience of future generations who want to start and end at the same car park! Consequently, at times there is no alternative to using the road; however almost always these are very quiet lanes on which you will probably meet no traffic. In some places there are beautiful wooden footpath signs but not the hint of a path on the ground. You have the choice of following the sign or going round the edge. If the ground is wet and ploughed we recommend avoiding picking up a couple of kilos of mud on each boot. If you do find blocked paths the relevant Rights Of Way officers would be pleased to know about them.

Maps. Numbers for the relevant Pathfinder maps are given for each walk with grid references for the starting point. If you are unfamiliar with maps, grid references are quite simple once you know how. The first 3 figures of the number refer to the numbers along the top and bottom of the map and the last 3 figures refer to those at the sides, so GR 234567 is read as 23.4 along the top or bottom and 56.7 up the side.

Suffolk County Council has a series of attractive walks leaflets obtainable from Tourist Information Centres or send an sae for a list and order form to The Environment & Transport Department, St. Edmund House, County Hall, Ipswich IP4 1LZ Tel: 01473 – 585658.

Transport. Almost all the walks can be reached at some point by bus but it can be very difficult to find buses running at suitable times. Although relevant bus company numbers are given it would be advisable to contact Suffolk Council Information Line who can help with co-ordinating bus routes. Tel: 01473 – 583358. Monday – Friday 8.45am – 6.00pm, Saturday 9.00am – 12.30pm.

Pubs. This is not a pub guide, so pubs have not necessarily been visited though comments appear where pubs were particularly enjoyed. Remember they do sometimes change hands. They are listed, with phone numbers for convenience. Unless the individual entry says otherwise they serve meals between 12noon and 2pm every day. Well behaved dogs on leads are generally welcome, or at least tolerated, in public bars but some pubs won't allow them on the premises — usually because they have their own dogs.

Churches. There are many lovely churches on these walks but no information about them appears in this book. There are so many really excellent books around on Suffolk churches that it seemed sensible to suggest you refer to any of them.

Equipment. Most of the walks are quite easy going underfoot but boots or stout shoes offer protection and even in a drought you can come across muddy patches, even if it's only from a crop irrigation system.

Further information. The Record Offices at Ipswich, Bury and Lowestoft hold many maps and documents if you want to go into things more deeply, and the staff are extremely helpful. Any of the Suffolk Wildlife Trust Publications are full of invaluable information. Some useful addresses are listed at the end of the book. There is also a selective bibliography of books used in researching this book. A visit to Ipswich Museum for its exhibits of the geology and wildlife of the area is recommended.

HISTORICAL BACKGROUND

SHAPING SUFFOLK

The skeleton of a landscape is forged by geological processes acting over aeons of time. Surface activity since the last glaciation
has put flesh on the skeleton, clothing it with topsoil and vegetation. In historic times the most important factor shaping the landscape has been farming.

Around 100 million years
ago the warm shallow seas
of the Upper Cretaceous
provided the chalk foun-
dations of what was, one
day, to become East
Anglia. This was overlaid
with London clay and
over the next several million years the sea levels
rose and fell and the
land surface gently tilt-
ed and folded.
Meanwhile the ice
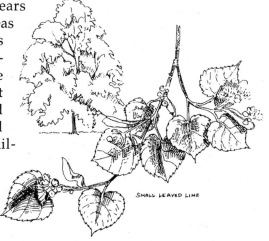
SMALL LEAVED LIME

sheets advanced and retreated, shaping and moulding the surface
of the land as they moved. In the warmer interludes vegetation
appeared, only to disappear under ice again. After the last glaciation, around 10,000BC, the Tundra-like vegetation sprang up once
more and as the climate continued to warm, gradually developed
into mature mixed forest. Around 8500BC birch gave way to pine
and hazel, then oak, small-leaved lime which became the dominant
tree in East Anglia, alder and various other deciduous species.
Finally the climate got so warm and wet that the sea level rose suf-
ficiently to cut the land bridge between Britain and the rest of
Europe — around 5000BC we became an island.

PREHISTORIC TIMES

Around 8300BC human beings concentrated in the light lands of the Sandlings and the Brecklands and along the river valleys. These early settlers were hunter gatherers and probably made little impact on the environment. From about 4600BC there is evidence of cereal and animal farming imported by immigrants from the low countries but originating from the Middle East.

The forest that covered East Anglia at this time was not wall to wall trees — it would have contained much open grassland with ponds and lakes. The sheep, goats and pigs belonging to the early settlers would help to keep the woods from growing too dense. As the population increased and agricultural practices developed, forest was cut back and burnt and the ground cultivated. As it lost its fertility it was abandoned and turned into heathland. The farmers moved on, felling more forest to provide more arable ground.

By the time of the Bronze Age the Sandlings and the Breckland would have had large areas of heath and grassland. Not until the

BRONZE AGE BARROW

9

Iron Age did people begin to settle the central woodland area, when belligerent tribes from the Ardennes brought a knowledge of iron working and broad bladed ploughs which they used to clear woodland and cultivate the heavy loam soils. Evidence of the activities of these early Bronze and Iron Age people has been found in barrows — burial or cremation mounds — of which there must have been many, appearing as tiny hills, dotting the landscape. They have now been almost completely flattened by centuries of ploughing. Isolated ones can be identified at ground level, often topped by a few trees, but from the air, crop marks give an idea of the extent of their original distribution.

ROMAN AND ANGLO-SAXON SUFFOLK

The Roman immigration which followed, lasted from AD43–425 and heralded an increasing domination of man over nature. A growing population led to increased land clearance for cultivation and building. Paved roads provided better communication and the creation of towns and ports with merchants and shopkeepers changed the nature of the rural economy. Specialized industrial production developed and numerous kilns were established, in the clay woodland areas that could also provide charcoal, to produce cheap crockery. Sand, flint and chalk were quarried for building materials. Farming flourished particularly in the brecks and fens of the west.

In the fifth century AD much of the Roman force withdrew, with disastrous effects on the economy; it must have been similar, in their terms, to the effect of the USAF withdrawal from the area in this century. Grass grew over abandoned towns and forts; peasants scratched a living, primitive conditions returned and the Dark Ages were born.

This dismal state of affairs continued, with sporadic invasions from Scandinavia, until continental trade began to pick up and Christianity arrived (around AD600–800). This late Anglo-Saxon period from AD850–1066 was very significant — for one thing it saw the birth of Suffolk. Until King Edmund was killed in AD869 what is now called Suffolk was that part of the Kingdom of East Anglia inhabited by the South folk. This period laid the foundations for the basic medieval economy to follow and in spite of the continual rampaging of the warlike Danes, Suffolk prospered and by the Norman Conquest was one of the most densely populated and intensively farmed regions of Britain.

MEDIEVAL SUFFOLK

In the ancient countryside of Suffolk arable land is thought, usually, to have been held in small compact blocks so fields tended to be small and irregularly shaped. There were large numbers of sheep, swine and goats, many of which were slaughtered every winter for lack of winter feed. Salt was needed to preserve the meat which led to the creation of salt pans on the coast and river estuaries. The Normans introduced a centralized regime and the church obtained vast estates. The manorial system of land enclosure and commoners' rights was introduced which allowed people to graze their animals and keep bees on the heaths and common land. They could cut bracken for animal bedding and thatch, heather for mattresses, walling, medicines and ale-making and gorse and turf for fuel. New hamlets and villages were founded and the land patterns established by Norman times were to last, recognisably, until almost the present day.

Woodland clearance continued during the 12th and 13th centuries. There was increasing enclosure of grassland and heath and by the 16th century most of the clayland of High Suffolk was enclosed by hedges and man-made ditches. Marshes fringing the rivers and coast were 'inned' with grass covered earth banks, behind which sheep and cattle grazed.

16TH TO 19TH CENTURIES

From the 16th–18th centuries dairying was the most important aspect of farming in Suffolk and great quantities of cheese and butter were produced and exported from its busy east coast ports. By the mid-19th century this dairy-based mixed farming had given way to arable — about 65 per cent of Suffolk's farm land was being ploughed including many permanent pastures in High Suffolk. Sheep were still an important farm animal throughout the county but with the greatest number of flocks being grazed on the light sandy soils of the Brecks and the Sandlings. During the 18th and 19th centuries heathland was ploughed and enclosed to make farms larger, more efficient and easier to work. Many farmers were eager to experiment with new crops, methods and technologies but battles with commoners arose over the loss of their rights.

20TH CENTURY

There have been enormous changes in farming in this century which have brought about fundamental changes in patterns of land use and so altered the look of the landscape, removing many traditional features.

In the early part of this century farming was in a poor state. It was more or less self-sustaining, relying on crop rotations with permanent pasture for horses, sheep and cattle which supplied manure for the crops. In the 1920s and 1930s the Forestry Commission bought up vast vistas of poor quality heathland and planted mile upon mile of, mainly, conifers in a bid to make the land productive and provide work. At the outbreak of the second world war Britain's farmers were producing only about 25 per cent of our food.

At the end of the war the government of the day vowed to see that Britain would never again have to rely on imports to feed her people and passed an Agricultural Act aiming to produce a stable and efficient farming industry. The impact on the Suffolk landscape has been dramatic. Farm Improvement schemes provided grants for reclaiming 'waste' land, ploughing up pastures, removing hedges, ditches, trees, banks and any other obstacles to intensive cultivation. Land was levelled, ditches, ponds and other depressions filled in to accommodate the mammoth machines built to work the vastly enlarged fields. Farmers became specialists, many growing only arable crops. Grassland declined from 30 per cent to 9 per cent in just over 40 years, reflecting the decline in cattle numbers by over 100 per cent since 1959. Poultry production doubled, but it was hidden away in vast factory-like sheds which are now common features in the landscape in some parts of the county. Sheep rearing has fluctuated according to grants available.

THE 1990S

In 1973 Britain became tied into the Common Agricultural Policy and the 1970s saw the height of production. Plant breeding led to strains giving higher yields; accurate application of a great spectrum of agro-chemicals became possible and it became the practice to work out in minute detail exactly how much of which nutrients to feed to livestock to provide the greatest growth for least cost. Bigger litters could be produced and even sometimes an extra litter in the year. Farming had really become an industrial process and this affected the look of the farming landscape. Great corrugated iron and asbestos hangers, enormous irrigation gantries, miles of rippling plastic sheeting took the place of clusters of wood, tile and thatched barns, trees, hedges and flower filled meadows. That may be a bit of a romantic exaggeration but this new prairie-like landscape was disliked by many and began to show its problems and shortcomings, especially soil erosion. As a result of this and the 'mountains' and 'lakes' of excess produce in the 1980s, conservation was 'discovered', fired the imagination and took off. Now we have a plethora of schemes known by their initials, all designed to protect, indeed even re-create, our vanishing traditional landscape.

Today (1997) things are improving. In spite of developing towns and road building over 80 per cent of Suffolk is still agricultural land, most of it farmed intensively, though a handful of farmers are farming in ways laid down by the Soil Association and other conservation minded bodies. Fortunately, however, there are other ways and means that farmers can improve the environment and produce a variety of habitats for wild life. Most of the government schemes seem to be having a positive effect though they suffer from insufficient funds.

Countryside Stewardship Scheme (CSS). Introduced in 1993. Its objectives are to sustain the beauty and diversity of the landscape; restore, improve and extend wild-life habitats and neglected landscape; conserve archaeological sites and historic features; improve opportunities for people to enjoy the countryside — though participants are not obliged to allow public access to their improved land.

Environmentally Sensitive Areas (ESAs). Introduced in 1987. Recognises that traditional livestock farming practices are important for the maintenance of landscape and wildlife habitats. In Suffolk there are three areas covering 23 per cent of the county: the Broads, Breckland and the Suffolk River Valleys. Farmers can obtain grants for similar purposes as under the Countryside Stewardship Scheme so that they can combine conservation and commercial farming using some traditional methods.

Set Aside. Introduced in 1989 as a means of reducing over-production but it can be used to enhance the environment. It came in two varieties, rotational and non-rotational. For example, earthworm numbers are very low in intensive arable land but will re-establish themselves in permanent pasture created with non-rotational set aside. Rotational set aside has not much environmental advantage as it may not be out of production long enough to

PARKLAND STREAM BED

change conditions. However tilling in spring instead of autumn provides winter stubble for food and shelter for birds and also helps prevent erosion.

Set Aside has been so successful in reducing over-production that it may be discontinued. Some of the other initials, SSSIs and CWSs — Sites of Special Scientific Interest and County Wildlife Sites respectively — offer protection to particularly fragile and valuable sites. Crucial as these schemes are for protecting endangered species they could result in mere oases of rare plants and animals. These plants and animals are the stuff of which countryside is made and they should exist all over it in their natural habitats. The schemes that encourage farmers to create and maintain a variety of habitats with corridors from patch to patch are, therefore, what is going to be vital in providing a rich, varied and living landscape.

LANDSCAPE FEATURES

HEDGES

In the early 19th century the poet John Clare complained that enclosure hedges were spoiling the wide open views and in 1851 Henry Stephen protested at the very bad hedge cutting he witnessed. Hedges were cut at about 3·5 feet to create a fence but of course all the new growth sprouted from around the cut area creating a "bush of thorn twigs on bare stakes." (Henry Stephen 'Book of the Farm' 1851). Large fields encourage the practice of flail mowing which chews instead of cutting the branches, allowing disease and decay to take hold. Some species die off, hedges become gappy and no longer serve the purpose of providing a windbreak or barrier to animals. A hedge that is coppiced or well laid need only be cut every 2 or 3 years to keep it thick and effective. Hedges that get a short back and sides every year never bear any fruit; they look boring and provide no food for dormice and songbirds who like to nest in untrimmed hedges. Many hedges arise naturally where plants have grown up along neglected fences and other boundaries.

In spite of massive hedge clearances in the 1960s and 70s, there are still remnants of ancient hedgerows in Suffolk, perhaps containing a dozen shrub species. They are living evidence of old field patterns and hence agricultural practices. As a rough guide to dating a hedge, count the number of species on both sides of a 30 yard stretch. It is likely to contain one shrub species for every 100 years of its existence. However it is not really as simple as that! Climate, soil type, farming regimes and what sources of seed there are nearby are important factors. Is there an upper limit to the number of species that will colonize a hedge regardless of its age? If the hedge is sinuous it is likely to be medieval. Post-1700 hedges tend to run in dead straight lines — any kinks are probably incorporated bits of older hedge. Pre-1720 maps of Suffolk show many hedgerow trees, and ancient hedges may also contain giant coppice stools or pollarded trees. Elm hedges may appear younger than they are; their strong invasive suckers tend to suppress other species. For serious hedge dating it is necessary to study early Ordnance Survey maps alongside current large scale ones, tithe maps and estate maps.

FIELDS AND COMMON LAND

Julian Tennyson, in his delightful book, 'Suffolk Scene' published in 1938 describes Suffolk fields as "so small", particularly in the east, with very varied contents and extraordinary shapes. They were concealed by hedges that were "fascinating, extravagant and dramatic ... anything that can find a place in them runs amok in a dizzy tangle."

Suffolk countryside is Ancient Countryside; that is it has mostly resulted from continuity and gradual, piecemeal adaptation over centuries rather than radical planning and modification, as in the Midlands, where the open fields were purposefully enclosed. Tom Williamson, writing in the journal of the Prehistory Society, however, says that removing medieval and post-medieval features from maps of High Suffolk shows up an underlying earlier planned landscape. But it is generally thought that open field systems in Suffolk were not common, were locally based and usually on the lighter soils.

What was grown in the fields before developments in agrochemicals and irrigation depended very much on the type of soil. Root vegetables and barley for malting suited the sandy soils of the Sandlings and the Breckland. Sheep have always

HEDGELESS
CROPFIELDS

been invaluable in the constant struggle to try and maintain a degree of fertility in these thin light soils. They grazed the summer grassland, manuring it before it was ploughed for winter wheat. Close folding of the ewes in winter prepared that land for planting spring barley.

The central clay plateau provided good corn growing fields and some excellent meadow land. In the 18th and 19th centuries the area including Stradbroke, Eye, Framlingham and Debenham was an important dairy district producing cartloads of butter for the London market.

The Anglo-Saxons introduced haymaking to provide animal feed during winter and managed their grasslands as either hay meadows or pastures. Grassland was considered more valuable than arable land throughout medieval times as it fed both livestock and working animals. By the 14th century it is probable that all the fertile river valley flood plains were hay meadows. Technically, meadows are grass fields used for haymaking and silage. Animals aren't put to graze on meadows till after haymaking. Pastures are grassland where animals are grazed from spring till autumn, they are not cut for hay. Ley farming, the planting of temporary pasture, declined in the late 18th, early 19th centuries, about the same time as clover was introduced and became common in arable rotation.

A great variety of crops were grown in the small fields of the county at the turn of the century. Peas, beans, turnips, carrots and kohl rabi fed both humans and animals, legumes improved the soil fertility. Wheat, barley, rye, oats, hops and flax were common. Sugar beet and oil seed rape now cover vast acres, flax has been reintroduced and in the lighter soils the ubiquitous carrot, asparagus, lettuce and soft fruit add to the variety of the fieldscape.

GREENS, COMMONS AND TYES

These are all names for common pasture lands. Across the clay plateau of High Suffolk they are generally called greens; commons in the north and east and tyes in the south — tye is an Essex term, an Old English word meaning small enclosure but in Suffolk, from the 13th century, it meant a large common pasture. There is however an overlap of terminology particularly amongst greens and commons in the east. Greens and tyes usually have houses round their edges. Commons around the east coast and in Breckland look more like heaths and have few, if any houses. Sutton Common, near Woodbridge, is the largest surviving one.

Greens come in all sizes, some large, long and rather erratically shaped like Wortham and Mellis. All Saints Common in South Elmham is another large 'green' partly unenclosed. Greshaw Farm and Common Road in this area testify to the past existence of Greshaw Green. For more about greens see the chapter on The Woodland.

WOOD PASTURE

This was pasture with trees, where the land and trees belonged to the Manor but commoners had grazing rights and could collect the wood. On tenanted land timber belonged to the landlord but tenants owned the wood from pollards, hence there tended to be a great many more pollards than timber trees! For wood pasture to survive a balance had to be struck between preserving the trees and animal grazing. Trees on the commons were often pollarded to prevent the livestock eating the shoots and leaves but sometimes the balance was lost and the pasture became a treeless common. At other times wood pastures were 'privatized', becoming parks or coppices.

MOATS, DIPS, PITS AND PONDS

There are some 740 medieval moated sites spread across the county, most enclosing under an acre. There are some considerably larger ones, for example South Elmham Hall. Many people are unaware of their existence as they tend to be sited well away from main roads. Although there are many intact moats surviving a lot have only one or two sides remaining; sometimes only a dry dip in the ground in front of a house shows where a moat once was. More information on moats in The Woodland chapter.

Walking through fields you will often see a tree-filled dip in the middle of the field; it is probably an old marl pit. Marl was any sub-

DISUSED MARL PIT

soil material, different from the top soil, that could be mixed with it to improve the condition of the land. For example sand and gravel added to a heavy clay top soil. Crag was used as marl in the Sandlings — crag pits look more like sand quarries and are home to sand martins. Marl pits were positioned in the middle of the field for convenience of carting. Clay pits were dug anywhere it was convenient, to use for sealing banks and river walls, building material and pottery. Brick pits come in various shapes and sizes, creating irregular holes and hills. Coprolite was a phosphate rich type of mudstone used as a fertilizer in the last century. Most of the open-cast type coprolite workings were filled in but some pits remain, such as the one opposite Newbourn Springs Nature Reserve — another haven for the sand martin. Gravel pits such as those in the Gipping valley have been turned into large lakes used for fishing and other recreational purposes. Flint mines — see the Breckland chapter.

Ponds can be natural or man-made; the latter were made for farm animals to drink from, for fishing or for industrial purposes, particularly in south Suffolk for processes used in the cloth industry. A lot of farm ponds were filled in in the 1950s and 60s when agricultural production was being intensified. Farmers, the Forestry Commission and the Wildlife Trust are now reinstating ponds but with the low rainfall of recent years many are drying out.

The earliest surviving earthworks are the Bronze Age burial mounds, concentrated in Breckland, south-east Suffolk, and along the river valleys. A few were in groups; the Seven Hills at Nacton, and about thirty stretching from Foxhall Heath across to Waldringfield. Iron Age folk also left burial mounds and forts but few have been identified; the ramparts at Clare are an example. Saxon burial mounds survive at Burrow Hill, Butley and Sutton Hoo.

WOODS, FORESTS, PARKS

The wildwood of prehistoric times was, in Suffolk, predominantly small-leafed lime and it is still the commonest tree of ancient woodland in the area between Ipswich, Sudbury and Stowmarket. Wildwood developed naturally; most native British trees don't like shade and won't grow under older trees of their own kind. When a tree dies or falls it creates a gap which may be filled by its own suckers, new growth or by seedlings from other nearby trees.

Very early on mankind began to manage the woodland. Bronze Age people used different thicknesses of rods and poles that appear to have been the result of coppicing. The Romans introduced sweet chestnut, a southern European tree, and they used a great deal of wood for their industries — iron, glass and brick making, grain drying and bathhouses. By around AD1200 much wildwood had been destroyed. Woods had been separated from each other, given defined boundaries and names, and many became privately owned. Woods were managed sustainably and from around AD1350 to the mid-19th century the economic value of woods and the cost of demolishing them tended to ensure their survival. Medieval woods had great economic importance, not just for their wood; bark was used for tanning, sap for pitch and tar, ash was used in potash, soap and glass. Pigs and other animals ate acorns and beech mast. Fences, ditches and banks were made to protect trees from browsing animals. Trees were grown to the size needed, not sawn up to fit as they are today and timber was felled for a specific job. A post mill for example required an oak 2 feet in diameter and 40 feet long.In the 18th century it became customary for a proportion of timber trees to be felled every year instead of just when the need arose.

The coming of the railways in the late 19th century, enabled the distribution of cheap coal and diminished the fuel wood market. Coppicing declined and plantations were introduced; often monocultures, they are planted and harvested like an arable crop, and came to be thought of as a financial operation. The first world war interrupted the import of foreign timber to Britain and the government responded by setting up the Forestry Commission which set about creating coniferous plantations with a vengeance.

Parks. The Medievals, to supply themselves with meat which they could hunt, created deer parks — fenced off clearings in wooded pastures — containing pollards and timber trees. In Tudor times the landscape aspects of parks developed, but it is the 18th century park that is renowned for its landscaping. Generally landscapers rearranged existing woodlands to enhance certain features such as particular ancient trees. They planted new trees, often exotic foreign species and created lakes. In some cases, such as Ickworth, the entire parish was swallowed up in the creation of the park but this had the effect of preserving the old trees and hedges.

Woodland Profile. Most ancient woods have the same shape they had 400 years ago, with sinuous or zig-zag boundaries, which could indicate additions from adjoining farmland. Where there were later additions the old boundary earthworks survive within the wood. Ridges and furrows on the woodland floor indicates wood-

FORESTRY COMMISSION PLANTATION

land that grew on previously ploughed fields. Dells, hollows and ponds, unless they have earth banks, are natural and may be the reason for the woods survival as the land was too pitted for easy cultivation. Medieval woodbanks were rounded or flat with massive ditches and pollarded trees. As time went by banks became smaller and more acutely angled. By the 19th century wood margins were, typically, straight with a small triangular bank and a single hawthorn hedge. Any wood with Monk, Nun or Prior in its name must have been around before the dissolution of the monasteries in 1536. Woods of recent origin bear names such as Plantation, Covert, Jubilee, Hundred Acre or Furze. Carr was a wood of alders, Spinney one of thorns.

Wood consists of underwood — basically the small stuff which is felled at more frequent intervals than timber. Timber trees, usually known as standards, are scattered amongst the coppice and may have originated from them, as suckers or grown from seed. Generally underwood and timber had different owners.

Trees and woodmanship. Trees do not have a predetermined life span. New wood is laid down annually from material produced by the leaves. Old age sets in when the tree can no longer form enough new wood to spread over the tree's surface. Branches begin to die back — the tree's strategy for retrenchment being to reduce the size of the crown —thus enabling the tree to share out its new wood over a smaller area. This produces stag head trees, which are not usually dying but have adapted to circumstances. Pollarding and coppicing of trees prolongs their life by providing a smaller area to be covered by new wood.

Coppiced woodland produces a distinctive flora of plants such as bluebells, primroses and wood anemones, needing alternate years of light to allow flowering and shade to suppress tall grasses that would otherwise smother them. In woods around Felsham there are stunning displays of the rare oxlip.

Recently there has been a considerable revival of woodmanship and coppicing and tree planting has run rife. New woods are being created on redundant farmland, for example Pound Farm Wood at Glemham. Oliver Rackham, in 'Trees and Woodland in the British Landscape', suggests this is not good conservation. Transplanted trees are, by definition, wounded trees which have a hard struggle to

NEW WOODLAND
POUND FARM
GLEMHAM

survive in the wild. They were 'born' and reared in a nursery and tend to be clone-like. Better to let existing trees spread — they provide variation.

It is difficult to kill established trees. The storm of October 1987 damaged mostly the conifer plantations. Rendlesham Forest was flattened but a few hundred yards up the road the ancient oaks and hollies of Staverton Thicks were barely touched. Most broken and uprooted trees were still alive and sprouting, some even continuing to grow in a horizontal position if they had a few roots left in the ground.

Dutch elm disease affects woodland elms more than those in fields and hedges. A Suffolk County Council survey in 1979 estimated that over 80 per cent of Suffolk elms were dead or diseased but elm suckers strongly and the survey also found many suckers, saplings and seedlings.

RIVER VALLEYS, MARSHES, FENS & HEATH

Suffolk is separated from Norfolk by the rivers Waveney and Little Ouse and from Essex by the Stour. Between these rivers the Blyth, Orwell, Deben and Alde/Ore/Butley system run into the North Sea.

The two rivers called Hundred and the Minsmere are silted up and form meres or trickle ignominiously into the sea. In the west, the Lark and the Little Ouse flow into the Wash via the Great Ouse. There is also a host of small rivers and streams running into the heart of Suffolk from the larger rivers. The Suffolk River Valleys have now been designated ESAs. This has protected a number of valuable marshland sites but it also aims to create new ones, to provide both water meadows and reed beds.

None of the rivers are in their natural state. Since at least the 17th century they have been dredged, diverted and dammed, straightened and chopped up by weirs and locks. They have been subject to industrial pollution, agricultural run-off and water abstraction. All this abuse has affected the quality and flow. The larger rivers were deepened and straightened to become 'navigations', to enable the transport of goods by barge. Now some river restoration is taking place and industrial pollution is much reduced. Some rivers are having their bends and narrows reinstated but low flow remains a problem. In the last 20 years an increasing population has demanded 30 per cent more water. More thirsty crops are being grown and irrigation machines working non-stop even during periods of rain, are a common sight. On top of this several years of exceptionally low rainfall have left many streams and some small rivers, such as the Kennet, so dry in places that grasses and other plants are growing on their beds.

Fens, unlike bogs, become waterlogged not just with rain but also from groundwater and surface run-off. They are less acid and have more nutrients, forming on a greater variety of soils, often derived from river silts. There are a number of small fen meadows along river valleys — Pakenham Fen is one example — but the valley fens have been decimated by drainage for agricultural reasons. The 230 hectares that remain along the upper Waveney Valley are SSSIs and of national importance. It is a fascinating and diverse landscape with reed and sedge swamp, alder and willow carr and grazed fen meadows, all supporting a rich diversity of wildlife.

Centuries ago the fens contained considerably more woodland. The wood and reeds were used for fuel and thatching and peat was dug for fuel: the pools at Redgrave Fen are old peat workings. This

REDGRAVE & LOPHAM
VALLEY FEN

use of the fenland vegetation helped maintain a diverse flora and fauna. Fenland reclamation began in Elizabethan times and the most north-westerly corner of the county is now drained, ditched, fertile agricultural land. More recently water extraction has lowered the water table causing drying out. Agricultural run-off and fertilizer drift have increased nutrients to the fens, and both have contributed to the disappearance of valuable plant communities. Two small restored fens can be seen on the Lakenheath walk, amongst the agricultural landscape.

Saltmarsh. The five shallow meandering estuaries are edged with varying amounts of saltmarsh and inter-tidal mud flats. Both have been much more extensive but saltmarsh reclamation began in medieval times for agricultural purposes and has continued ever since. Though marsh land is no longer reclaimed for agriculture — in fact some arable land is being deliberately flooded to re-create marsh — it is being extensively used for the creation of marinas and industrial use. Most notably the Port of Felixstowe has swamped acres of saltmarsh and mudflats. The Orwell, the most industrialized of the rivers, has lost half its saltmarsh in the last 150 years but the Deben has increased its area by an appreciable amount, largely because of breaches in the sea wall.

Saltmarshes develop on sheltered mudflats, above the mean high water of neap tides, when wave energy dissipates over the mud, allowing sediments to settle. Gradually a few plants take hold which trap more sediment and help reduce the effects of the wave action. As the surface builds up, more and different plants colonize the growing marsh. Further information on saltmarsh, mudflats and shingle banks can be found in the Sandlings chapter.

Heathland. The lowland heaths of Suffolk have come about largely as a result of human activity. Early farmers cut down woodland to grow their crops, interrupting the natural circulation of nutrients through the vegetation and soil fauna. Crop plants withdrew nutrients from the soil and rain water leached what was left from the decomposing plant remains on the surface down through the mineral layers below, leaving a nutrient deficient podzol. Just the sort of soil heather thrives on. Heathers and other heathland plants moved into these areas mainly from nearby woodland glades.

Not all heathland is heather although it is the dominant vegetation in the dry acid Sandlings heaths which are very poor in plant species. Heather won't grow in shade and it does not compete well on a nutrient rich soil — other plants flourish and it is shaded out. Breckland heaths are very different, being a complex mixture of acid sand and calcareous chalk soils. They have a very rich flora including many downland plants.

The total area of heathland in Suffolk today is about 3,500 hectares. Sixty years ago is was about 42,000 hectares. It is very fragmented : about 70–80 fragments varying in size from 570 hectares at Lakenheath Warren to bits of less than 2 hectares.

Heathland management is all about diverting natural succession and grazing has always been a very important means of keeping down the growth of unwanted plants, as place names including Warren and Walk testify. Bracken is particularly hard to control; it has an extensive underground root system and will send up shoots a great distance from the parent plant. It can be cut, but to destroy it means cutting about 4 times a year for several years and this is not practical on a grand scale. When cut, the fronds must be removed or they will rot and provide nutrients that encourage the growth of further shoots and other plants that will compete with heather. Not many animals like to eat it — Beulah sheep are a notable exception and the Wildlife Trust have flocks of sheep which are moved around the heathlands to help with the control of bracken and birch scrub.

ROADS, LANES, AND TRACKS

Many of the tracks of prehistoric settlers can now only be deduced from aerial photographs of crop marks, though later settlers clearly used and 'modernized' existing tracks, successors of which are still in use today. Very early on a network of tracks across the county was used for importing and exporting goods from the area, and for the military activities of the various Iron Age tribes who were a pugnacious lot.

It was, of course, the Romans who started building paved roads. On the heavy clay of mid-Suffolk it required a formidable amount of digging and drainage and many of these routes, or signs of them, remain. However on the light soils of the Sandlings little survives, possibly because the light quickly draining sands did not require foundations.

About 400 miles of Roman road can be identified on modern maps of Suffolk. The Roman road from Coddenham to Ixworth, via the Gipping and Blackbourn valleys, was a forerunner in parts to the present A14. Roman Pye Street is now the A140 Ipswich to Norwich Road. These were built for strategic military reasons but roads were also built to connect settlements and markets. Numerous tracks and lanes were worn by people travelling between villages, fields and farms or by driving sheep and cattle to pasture. Cattle tracks in particular are winding and tend to keep to the margins between different sorts of farmland, particularly bordering marshland. A good example can be found on the Redgrave–Wortham walk. This cattle track runs from Diss to Redgrave via Low Road and Fen Street, then on to Thelnetham and Hopton where it crosses the marshy valley and returns along the north side of the river to Diss.

A 16th century Act of Parliament made parishes responsible for the upkeep of roads but since many were unwilling or unable to do so, further Acts in the mid-17th century enabled Turnpike Trusts to be set up with the power to build toll gates and collect tolls. In

OLD HUNDRED LANE
NEAR STONHAM ASPALL
EARLY 10th CENTURY

Suffolk these roads are still our major routes — the A14, A140, A12 for example. These turnpikes did not please cattle drovers. They did not want to pay the tolls and anyway cattle needed to graze en route. Therefore any lanes and minor roads that run more or less parallel to a turnpike can be suspected of being old drove roads.

Present day tracks running alongside parish boundaries are probably ancient and where a pattern emerges of roads, tracks and paths converging on a pond or common this may well indicate very ancient ways.

Roadside verges which were once rich grassland, even semi-woodland in places, have been cut and sprayed for the benefit of car drivers and crops. However a more enlightened approach to cutting the banks in recent years has led to the return of flowering plants such a snowdrops, primroses, cowslips and mallow. Many verges containing plants once common in herb rich grassland are now nature reserves, protected by the Suffolk Wildlife Trust and the County Council. These strips, marked at either end with white posts labelled Roadside Nature Reserve, are cut once a year after flowering. There are around 100 such sites across the county, harbouring a variety of insects as well as interesting plants.

BUILDINGS AND PEOPLE

Churches, castles, domestic and farm buildings were made from local materials available at the time they were built. In the Middle Ages stone was only imported for particularly important buildings such as monasteries. Orford Castle and the church tower were built from septaria, a local mudstone, and local coralline crag was used in the church towers at Wantisden and Chillesford. Clay was commonly used for cottages and farm houses, mixed with straw, fashioned into large blocks and sun dried. It was also mixed with horsehair and dung to provide 'daub' for infilling 'wattle'— hazel rods used in the walls of timber framed houses. The timber came from local oak trees and the walls were plastered over. The traditional Suffolk pink colour of the plaster was said to be obtained by adding sloe juice or ox blood, depending who you believe. Decorative pargeting came in at the end of the 17th century and there are some good examples in and around Hadleigh. Clay was also made into bricks from an early date and at first they were probably made on the building site. In the 16th century they became a more popular material and were used decoratively in herring-bone patterns, for example, as seen in Laxfield and Fressingfield. The characteristic white bricks of Woolpit are common in houses in that area and also in Ipswich where they seem to have been used a great deal in Victorian times. Until the end of the 17th century most buildings were thatched, using Norfolk reeds with wheat or rye straw for the ridges. After this, peg-tiles became common, then pantiles, made at the many brickworks in the county. An odd brick construction, characteristic of Suffolk is the crinkle-crankle wall, mostly built in the 19th century. In the north of the county flint was readily available; flint pebbles being used to build walls and cut, or knapped, flints used decoratively as flushwork on churches and other important buildings.

Apart from a few Saxon towers buildings must have kept a very 'low profile' in the landscape, till the Normans started building church towers and castles. Until the middle of the 20th century very little would have shown above the trees giving the landscape a much less man-made appearance than today.

Windmills providing power to grind corn, were once a common sight across the county; one of the earliest recorded being at Bury in the 12th century. Most of the windmills still around today date from the mid-18th to mid-19th centuries when mills were very important, but they may well have been built on sites of earlier mills. There were over 400 working mills in Suffolk in the early 19th century. The earliest mills

DRINKSTONE POST MILL 1689

were post mills — the whole mill turned round a central post, to catch the wind. At the end of the 18th century tower mills became more common. Only the cap and sails turned, on a fixed brick tower. Windmills were also used to drain marshland along the coast and in the fens.

Watermills were also an important feature since the earliest times, though not as widespread as windmills. There were 95 working watermills in the 1850s; mostly used for grinding corn but also in the manufacture of textiles and silk spinning. These mill buildings all had their accompanying mill ponds; 3 were powered by the tide. Towards the end of the 19th century the availability of steam engines put paid to windmills and in due course to watermills as well but a number of the buildings can still be seen around the county, some in operation as a tourist attraction.

People. A feature of todays landscape that must have been very different even a few decades ago, is its emptiness of people. I have often walked for hours without setting eyes on another human being. The fields are burgeoning with beautiful glossy upright beet leaves, feathery carrot ferns or swathes of thick golden corn, and barely a weed in sight. They look so well cared for but you rarely see anyone caring for them. You only have to look at a book of old photographs to see fields full of people doing things. In bygone centuries the countryside presented a busy landscape filled with peasants and animals, like a Brueghel painting.

BRECKLAND

In 1735 John Kirby referred to three regions of Suffolk as the Woodlands, the Sandlands and the Fielding — the latter being the last area to retain its open fields. In the late 19th century the Fielding was renamed Breckland from the old Norwegian 'braec', land newly broken for cultivation then left to regain fertility. It stretches from just north of Bury to Mildenhall in the west and Swaffham in the north. Only a third of its 370 square miles is in Suffolk. Like the Sandlings it has shallow acidic sandy soils but being further inland has a more extreme, continental climate. The ice of the last Ice Age stretched south to the Norfolk coast causing permafrost throughout Breckland. When the ice retreated about 10,000 years ago the melt water dissolved fissures in the surface chalk. Winter frosts widened the cracks which later filled with drifting sand and silt forming odd shaped pockets of soil which show up in surface variations on some ploughed land and in heathland vegetation. The chalky patches produce chalk downland plants, with lime-hating plants colonizing the acid soil in the cracks.

Julian Tennyson described a breck as an area of bare, stony, sandy soil, devoid of all but sorrel, ragwort, bugloss and meagre grass; miles of heathland and large areas of forest. He felt it to be a place of desolation, whose strange, sometimes sinister, nature held a feeling of latent power which he could not understand, yet found "fascinating". He also found — in 1938 — 27 villages that could not raise a pint of beer between them!

SPECIAL FEATURES

Scots pines. Relatively sparse tree cover emphasises the presence of the Scots pines. They stand in rows between fields or in clumps atop tumuli. First planted as windbreaks over 200 years ago, often cut back to form hedges during the enclosures, gnarled fragments still survive. They grow fast in the poor light soil, binding it with their roots and helping to protect against blown sand drifting over the fields and heaths.

Warrens. Now only commemorated by names on a map, Breckland was once covered with warrens, each of several thousand acres. There were warrens at Brandon, Lakenheath, Wangford, Eriswell and Mildenhall. They were enormously important to the economy from the 12th century, when the Normans introduced rabbits to this country, up until earlier this century when so many rabbits had escaped to the wild that there was no point in farming them any more. These early rabbits, imported from the warm Mediterranean, did not take kindly to life in Britain and had to be nurtured and cossetted by the monks and the gentry who regarded them as a gastronomic delight!

From the 18th century warrens were often walled with great earth banks. Fortified lodges were built where the warrener could keep a look out for poachers and watch to see the rabbits didn't escape and damage the crops. They also had to wage a constant war with predators and birds of prey.

The mid-13th century warren at Lakenheath was maintained right up until the second world war when the Ministry of Defence took over a large part of it for the airfield, still in use. After a setback during the first world war it continued to produce thousands of rabbits a year, both for the table and the skin trade.

On the other side of the A1065 road from the airfield next to the grassy remains of **Lakenheath Warren** is **Wangford Warren** now part of Thetford Forest. **Wangford Warren Nature Reserve**, a mere slither of lichen heath and sand dunes, just north of the airfield is the only remaining example of the open sand dune system that once covered the whole warren area where constant rabbit grazing kept this heathland dune system looking the way Wangford Warren does today. In 1668 an enormous sandblow from here nearly buried the village of **Santon Downham** and partially blocked the Little Ouse. A field next to the reserve is being allowed to revert to heath and the whole area plus a neighbouring fen will be grazed by sheep, thus reinstating a piece of typical Breckland landscape.

SCOTS PINE HEDGE

Cavenham Heath National Nature Reserve is a very important surviving example of Breckland heath, rich in flora and fauna and giving an idea of how much of Breckland must have looked right up to the beginning of the 20th century.

Flint, a kind of chert formed from microscopic marine organisms and mineral silica, occurs in layers in the chalk which outcrops in the Breckland area. It has proved useful for a number of purposes the most obvious of which, to the visitor to the area, is as a building stone. Churches, houses, barns, walls all built of, or decorated with, local flint. Walking through the more chalky fields you notice lumps of flint of various sizes strewn around. The Romans probably gathered flints from the fields to build their walls, but 2000 or so years previously Neolithic people were already mining flint a few miles north at **Grimes Graves**, an area containing 700–800 pits and shafts, some as much as 14 metres deep and up to 8 metres wide. The best quality flint, known as floorstone, occurs about 12 metres down so mining techniques were developed to excavate galleries radiating out from the main shaft. Digging was done with picks made from red deer antlers and the sand and chalk spoil was used as infill. The flints were skilfully fractured into smaller pieces to form tools and weapons. With the advent of bronze and iron working flint implements became redundant and Grimes Graves closed down around 1000BC. Flint continued to be used in building and later on it became an essential component of flintlock guns. Flint mines were dug on Lingheath at the south eastern edge of Brandon and the town became the gunflint capital of the British Empire. The arrival of percussion guns put an end to this industry but there are a few flint knappers today supplying the building industry and gun clubs.

Earthworks and early settlements. Once numerous, earthworks have mostly been flattened or buried. Icklingham was a major Roman settlement and there are traces of a number of Roman villas along the River Lark. The area was settled long before the Romans however, and there are still Bronze Age burial mounds to be seen. Hoards of Bronze Age artefacts have been found around Lakenheath and Wangford. Evidence of Iron Age and Roman settlements have been found in Thetford Forest around High Lodge and flint and metal implements, bits of pots and querns dating from the Stone Age onwards have been found in many places. Part of the, probably, Saxon Black Ditches system runs through fields near Icklingham. At West Stow Country Park there is a reconstruc-

SAND DUNES AT WANGFORD WARREN

tion of an Anglo-Saxon village and there would have been similar villages scattered over Breckland between approximately AD420 and AD650.

On the high ground between Lakenheath village and the airfield, more recent earthworks, old sand and gravel pits now overgrown with scrub, grass and flowers, provide an attractive recreational area.

LAND SETTLEMENT AND FARMING

From various archaeological finds and from pollen analysis it has been deduced that Neolithic settlers grew wheat and barley in this area for two or three consecutive years then grazed their sheep or cattle on the land to rest it, restore fertility and prevent it being colonized by heath and scrub. When they moved on, the heathland re-established itself behind them.

After them the Romans and the Anglo-Saxons continued the settlement of the banks of the River Lark. They also continued sheep and cattle grazing and arable farming, and by the Middle Ages farming systems were firmly based on sheep. Very large flocks of long legged Norfolk sheep roamed the almost barren wastes by day and were folded at night on arable land. In the early 13th century the climate warmed up and new areas of heathland were broken up for cultivation. The land became overcultivated, overgrazed and impoverished. In 1300 a dreadful sandstorm buried some 30 villages and by the end of the century frequent, extensive sandstorms defeated the villagers — they gave up, abandoning marginal land and deserting villages.

Rabbit farming continued although rabbit grazing added to the sandblow problems. With the dissolution of the monasteries local families bought up the monastic land. Some bought whole villages and smallholders had to move away. By the end of the 17th century the area was quite seriously depopulated.

18th & 19th Centuries. The situation improved during the Napoleonic wars (1790–1815). Many new farms were built on heaths and warrens, partly encouraged by the Enclosures Acts. A modified Norfolk four crop rotation followed marling. Turnips, barley, ley for two years, rye then back to turnips. Cattle kept in yards in the winter churned straw into manure which was then spread on the fields. The main problems persisted: rabbits and dry years. During the 19th century the wild population of rabbits increased to pest proportions, often devastating winter sown corn. Commercial rabbit farming declined and cheap grain was beginning to come in from America. Cereal growing in Breckland became unprofitable and land went out of production and reverted to heath. Some unemployed farm workers got work on the railway being built through Brandon but the railway almost put paid to the horse drawn barge traffic on the rivers, which since the Middle Ages had transported wool, coal, brick, corn, salted rabbit meat and timber to the ports.

20th century. By the time the 1930s depression set in about the only source of income in Brandon was felt-making from rabbit skins. Women prepared the skins at home and sold the trimmings for making shoddy. Around 4 million skins a year were used but the industry, like the rabbits, was killed off by myxomatosis.

After a brief revival during the first world war, farming became very depressed in the 1920s. New crops were introduced such as sugar beet, the long tap roots of which overcame the dry soils to some extent and asparagus which suited the free draining soils. From the 1930s to the 1970s a great deal of asparagus was grown, mainly in the breck soil, whilst chicory was grown extensively in the peaty fen soil. In 1965 Lakenheath had the largest chicory factory in Europe, providing chicory to mix with coffee essences. It closed in 1981 and is now a carrot packing plant. Also in the 1930s Bryant and May Forestry planted acres and acres of black poplars on the poorly drained fen. After WW2 the land was drained to grow food crops and the poplars dwindled to 100 acres.

In the 1950s there was a revival and Lakenheath had the largest poplar forest in Britain. Unfortunately Bryant and May found they could get timber more cheaply elsewhere and sold up. But the demand for matches was decreasing; most of the poplars were uprooted and the land used for arable farming. During WW2 much of the remaining heathland had been deeply ploughed to bury the heather and bracken, then dosed with massive quantities of lime to make it suitable for growing food crops. Following the demise of the rabbits crops could be grown in places where they would not have survived the ravages of the rabbits and yet more heath was ploughed up.

Modern times. Most of the heathland cultivated at that time is still being used for arable land though Breckland is now an Environmentally Sensitive Area with grants available to return the land to heath and grassland and to farm it in traditional ways. Another introduction since the war has been irrigation from river and stream extraction and underground boreholes. This has greatly expanded the range of crops that can be grown, especially vegetables. Machinery can easily be used after rain on these free draining soils which makes it possible to provide carrots almost all the year round with regular supplies of other fresh vegetables. The first carrot crop is planted in January under polythene, for lifting in May. Later varieties are continually planted and the last lot is covered with straw in the autumn for pulling in January. It requires vast investment in machinery and agrochemicals, to produce the perfect carrot demanded by supermarkets. Carrot growing was moved from the black fen soil to the sandy Brecks because customers, so the supermarkets said, didn't like dirty marks on their carrots! The small farmer cannot afford to compete so only the very large growers are left. Potatoes are also grown on a large scale and of course asparagus. Linseed, oil seed rape, evening primrose and borage paint the fields in

CHICORY

varying shades of blue and yellow. Wheat can only be grown on the better soils but both rye and winter sown barley do well and are ready before summer droughts set in.

Large poultry factories stand out in the flat landscape — the manure from which goes to the arable farmers or to the Eye Electricity generator — an imaginative way of disposing of large quantities of chicken manure but not popular with local residents! There is some traditional duck farming and outdoor pigs are increasingly fashionable, their mini Nissen huts, known as arks or igloos, being moved around to prevent disease but this also ensures that the land is evenly manured and churned up. Sheep are mostly confined to heath and rough grazing where they do a most valuable job in keeping bracken and other undesirable plants in check. In the autumn they are folded in fields of arable by-products, such as old cabbage stalks, to fatten.

Breckland Rivers. The Wissey, the Lark and the Little Ouse, are all small high quality chalk streams which continue to run in times of drought. They flow into the Great Ouse and so on to the Wash. The construction of Denver Sluice on the Great Ouse in 1652 adversely affected the flow and the rivers began to silt up causing problems for laden barges which needed 1.5 metres of water. A primitive kind of lock called a staunch, a kind of gate suspended over the river and raised and lowered on a chain, was used. It was very slow and could be dangerous but it was cheap to install and made navigation possible. The remains of some staunches can be seen at St Helen's picnic site in Santon Downham and in West Stow Country Park.

Earlier this century Breckland rivers and streams were straightened and canalised. Now they are being bent again and in places croys — lumps of flint — are put into the stream to narrow the channel, thus speeding up the water flow and causing ripples and pools. This oxygenates the water making it possible for a greater variety of wildlife to live in it. Otters which disappeared in the 1970s have been succcessfully re-introduced.

Forestry. After the first world war farming in Breckland was in a parlous state and unemployment was high. All this led to the Forestry Commission, created because of the national timber short-

WINTER VEGETABLE FIELD

age, starting to plant the largest lowland pine forest in the country — 20,000 hectares. Farmers were glad to sell their land to the Forestry who used local labour to build roads, clear scrub and exterminate the rabbits.

Seeds, collected by local work gangs from trees already growing in the area, were planted in nurseries within the forest and transplanted by hand where they were to grow. At peak times 7 million seedlings a year were produced. Pines did best but for cosmetic reasons broad leafed trees and larch were planted round the edges. After 16–20 years thinning starts and continues at 4–6 year intervals, leaving only 150 trees to reach maturity from every 2000 planted. By the 1960s the forest was in full production and the Brandon depot was handling up to 125,000 cubic metres of timber a year. But demand for timber declined; the knock on effect of pit closures and modern mining methods. In 1988 it closed. In 1991 high tech mechanisation was introduced which could harvest 250 trees a day. The stumps are removed and bulldozed into windrows to rot and return nutrients and organic matter to the soil. Seedlings are now planted by machinery though regular thinning is still done in the traditional manner. The trees are sprayed with fungicides and pesticides and the ground with herbicides as necessary. The timber is processed in mills throughout eastern England.

Although Thetford forest is very much a working forest and large areas of it are used by the military and so out of bounds to the public, the Forestry Commission has done a lot to make the forest accessible to everyone for recreation.

NATURAL HISTORY

Centuries of cultivation turned the Breckland area from rather sparsely wooded forest into a mosaic of heathland, arable farmland, forest and river valleys. This century with the intensive mechanisation of farming and the dictates of supermarkets, much of the area is covered in vast fields though there are smaller fields and there are good hedges. The movement of wildlife about the fragments of heathland has been very effectively blocked by the extensively farmed land and by plantations of trees. Rabbits are now not always numerous enough to deal with the birch and bracken, though **Cavenham Heath** is fortunate in having a good number of rabbits providing areas of short turf and areas where stags-horn lichen thrives. Many lichens are doing well here, perhaps because the heather *Calluna vulgaris* which needs around 23 inches of water a year to flourish, is dying back and not regenerating, leaving bare patches which lichens colonize.

Seventy-five per cent of Breckland heath has been lost in the last hundred years but there is now some protection in the form of National Nature Reserves, SSSI status and the Norfolk and Suffolk Wildlife Trusts. It is they, very largely, who try to keep the heaths and river valleys in a fit state for the proper diversity of wildlife which would naturally live there.

On the chalky grassland soils flowers typical of downland pasture, such as birds foot trefoil, thyme, common rock rose, quaking grass, and eyebright grow, as well as common spotted, pyramidal and twayblade orchids. On the verges and footpaths you can find vipers bugloss, mullein, dyers greenweed, soapwort and musk mallow.

Animals. Red squirrels were very numerous until the 1920s. Now only a few can be found in **Thetford Forest** where they are being studied under the Species Recovery Programme and being bred in captivity and released. There are around 4,000 fallow deer but only 150 each of red, roe and muntjak: 400–500 deer are culled annually to ensure herds are healthy and balanced for males and females. Adders and grass snakes are quite common and bats are being encouraged.

Birds. Cavenham and **Weeting Heaths** have the largest concentration of stone curlews in Britain — 92 pairs in 1993. There were 1,000 pairs in 1940. They return to the same nesting sites year after year and so keen are farmers to conserve them that they will drive round them when ploughing the fields where they are nesting. In the pine forests are brambling, siskin, tits of all sorts, turtle doves, goldcrests, firecrests and crossbills. Oak, sweet chestnut,beech and larch provide wonderful autumn colour and attract hawfinches, nuthatches, warblers, coal, long tailed and willow tits. A policy of clear felling a proportion of the forest each year provides heathlike patches which encourage wheatear, whinchat, stonechat, meadow pipit, woodlark, nightjar and red legged partridge, to be followed by songbirds such as yellow hammer, whitethroat and tree pipit when nettles and scrub start to grow. Dead tree trunks are left for spotted woodpeckers to nest in and for birds of prey to perch on. Hobby, kestrel, sparrowhawk, jay, magpie, tawny and long eared owls nest in thinned pines. Rivers provide breeding sites for a variety of ducks, kingfishers and mute swans.

A rather surprising benefactor of wildlife in the brecks has been the military, who since the beginning of the century have had a battle training ground here. In the second world war there were 8 active airfields and 3 dummy ones complete with toy planes. The MOD expanded their holding in 1990. They started building replicas of 'enemy' scenes, checkpoints and villages with Russian tanks. Then glasnost arrived before it was finished! Eight hundred sheep graze the battle area and are corralled during firing. All firing and other warlike activities stop for 4 weeks during the lambing season. No pesticides or herbicides have been used in the battle area so natural succession has occurred and the area has become a haven for wildlife and a designated SSSI. There are over 600 flower and plant species including 28 rarities; 331 moth species and 28 butterfly species; 137 bird and 26 mammal species, none of which seem to mind military activity.

FEN

The parishes of Lakenheath and Mildenhall, which border on Cambridgeshire and Norfolk, lie on the boundary of fen and breck, where the sand of the Breckland dips under the peat of the fen basin. The Fens were once an extension of The Wash, forming a large inland sea with low islands. Mildenhall and Freckenham formed the Suffolk shore. Much of the area around Lakenheath and Mildenhall would have looked like the nature reserves at Lakenheath before the Drainage Act of 1759. Since then, many further drainage schemes and intensive farming have made the fen and breck look more like each other. Draining of farmland is still causing the fens to dry out and some rare plants such as bogbean and bog myrtle have disappeared completely though other uncommon wetland plants are hanging on, such as sneeze-wort, yellow loosestrife and marsh stitchwort. Pashford Poors and Lakenheath Poors Fens are so called because the poor of the parish could cut peat for fuel and reeds for thatching and bedding. The last peat was dug in the 1920s.

STONE CURLEW

1. LAKENHEATH FENS

An easy walk along wide sandy or grassy tracks over pleasant fen land, including two nature reserves of fen meadow and fen valley habitats. Lakenheath is on the borders where fen and breck meet.

Distance: 11 km (7 miles) or 5.5 km (3.5 miles).

Map: Pathfinder 942.

Start: Wings Road car park off Lakenheath High Street. GR 713828.

Buses: Services from Bury. Eastern Counties Tel. 01284–766171.

WHERE TO EAT
Several pubs in the middle of the High Street and one a bit off the centre.
Half Moon, 4 High St., Tel. 01842–861484.
Lakenheath Bakery attached to a garage in the High Street and the delicatessen at the other end of the street sell freshly filled rolls, cakes etc.

LOCAL INTEREST
At first glance, apart from the impressive church set in a large lime tree lined churchyard, Lakenheath may not seem too appealing but it has some interesting history. In medieval times it was a market town and on the line of an ancient droving route skirting the edge of the Fens. Barges sailed from the quays on Lakenheath Lode to the Little Ouse river and thence to The Wash. There were a number of pits for chalk, clay, sand and gravel. Hard chalk was used for walling; soft chalk, burnt in kilns to produce quick lime, was used in mortar or slaked and spread on the land. The flint used for walling is evident throughout the area. Clay pits provided clay to maintain flood walls. Several gravel pits graced Lakenheath Warren, the gravel being exported from Lakenheath Lode. Many of the old workings have been left to grow over, making a very attractive area on the high ground to the east of the town with views over the airfield to Thetford Forest.

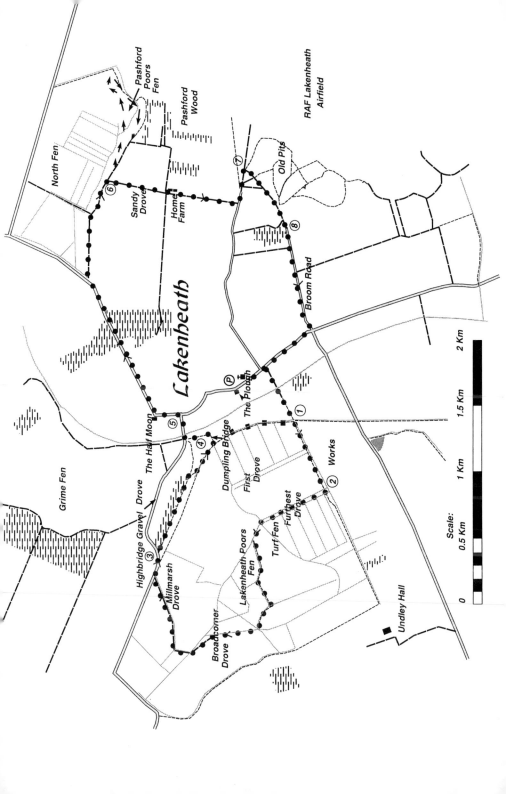

Pashford Poors Fen and Lakenheath Poors Fen. So called because the poor of the parish could cut peat for fuel and reeds for thatching and bedding. The last peat was dug in the 1920s. Now both are SSSIs and in the care of the Suffolk Wildlife Trust. They contain fen meadow and valley fen habitats and show what much of the fens would have looked like in times gone by.

Wangford Warren Nature Reserve (SWT). Sand dunes and lichen heath. Rare breeding birds so access restricted in spring and summer. GR 756842.

WALK: Turn left down the High Street. About 100 yards past the church, opposite the Chinese Restaurant, turn right on to a narrow grassy path (signposted) which leads to stiles either side of a bridge over the flood relief channel. It becomes a broad track. Follow it straight ahead.

1. Cross a junction of four tracks and past the waste paper works (behind a high bank.)

2. Turn right onto a stony track (Furthest Drove) leading across Turf fen. In less than half a mile you come to Lakenheath Poors Fen grazed by rather baleful looking cows. There is a stile into the fen and an information board by it. Past the Fen the walk continues on private farm tracks, with the owners kind permission. Follow the broad attractive tracks of Broadcorner Drove and Millmarsh Drove to the road.

3. Turn right and follow the waymarked track between two fields, heading towards the church tower. It goes up on to the dyke wall and broadens out.

Very pleasant track with views across attractive fenland. Lots of butterflies and wildflowers, e.g birds foot trefoil, common toadflax, white silene, hemp agrimony out in September. To the

BLACK BOG RUSH

left you can see the chalk merging with the black fen soil.

At the end of the dyke wall follow the track ahead past 2 more fields.

4. Turn left to Dumpling Bridge, then cross the channel at Highbridge Gravel Drove.

5. Turn left into the High Street. Passing the Half Moon pub on your left follow the road for about 1 kilometre and where it bends to the left take the broad gravel track to the right. Follow this to Pashford Poors Fen, the information board will identify it. You can walk all round the fen but to continue the walk retrace your steps to the footpath, signed to the left — Sandy Drove.

GREAT FEN SEDGE

6. Follow this broad track to a metalled lane, making a T junction; turn left and after about 100 metres there are 2 sandy tracks going over rough grass to the right. Pass these and take the next path to the right.

7. At the top of the rise bear right towards the enclosure surrounding an aerial. Turn left and follow the track almost to where the houses start.

8. Branch off to a footpath down the left side of the pines, parallel with the track you have left. Follow it to the made up road (Broom Road) into town.

You may wander the many paths that meander amongst the dips and rises of the old sand and gravel pits, now attractively overgrown with grass, flowers, lichen, rushes and scrub. Harebells and evening primrose were flowering in September.

SHORT WALK: avoiding roads. Start as above to **(3)** Continue straight ahead to **(1)**, turn left and over the bridge to the High Street; left back to the car park.

2. Thetford Forest

This route is just one suggestion, there are numerous rides and paths in the forest and you are free to wander anywhere provided there are no notices asking you to keep out because of forestry activity. The forest produces 200,000 tonnes of timber a year so there is always work going on somewhere. Don't rely on the OS maps, they may be out of date.

All the paths are good, sandy or grassy and level. Pleasant woodland scenery with some interesting wild flowers and birds, even a red squirrel may be seen. Very pretty along the river; views from the higher spots. Santon Downham village — forestry houses round a very large attractive village green.

Distance: 8.75km (5.5 miles).

Map: Pathfinder 942 and 943.

Start: Santon Downham — Forest Office car park. GR 818877.

Buses: from Bury, Brandon, Newmarket and Thetford. Eastern Counties. Tel. 01284–766171.

WHERE TO EAT
High Lodge Forest Centre cafe.
Santon Downham village shop by car park.
Three formal picnic sites and numerous informal ones.
Brandon, several pubs and cafes e.g. **Brandon House Hotel,** Tel. 01842–810171; **Great Eastern,** Tel. 01842–814236; **Bridge House Hotel,** Tel. 01842–813137; all do teas.

LOCAL INTEREST
High Lodge Forest Centre. Evidence of Iron Age and Roman settlements found here. Was a forestry labour camp in the 1930s. Shop, cafe, toilets, various family activities. Sell orienteering maps. Open daily 10am – 5pm Easter to end September. Winter opening details Tel. 01842–810271.
Brandon Country Park. Woodland and landscaped grounds, lake and Victorian walled garden. Visitor Centre with good displays about Breckland natural history. Picnic sites and walks. Toilets.

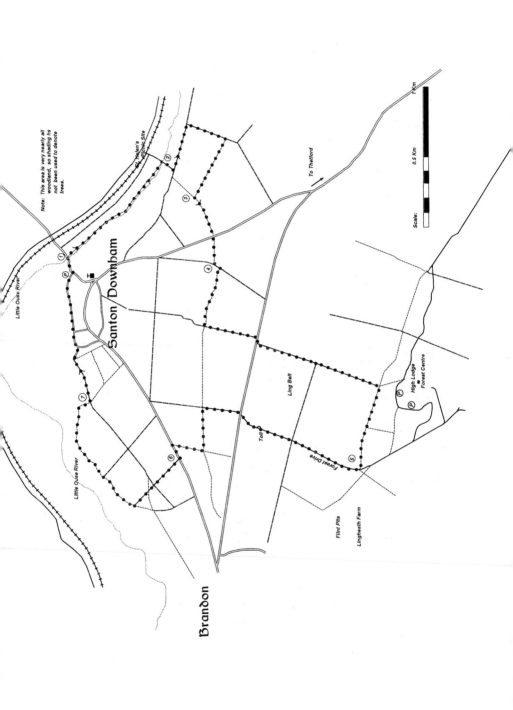

Note: This area is very nearly all woodland, so shading its not been used to denote trees.

Little Ouse River

St. Helen's Picnic Site

Santon Downham

To Thetford

Little Ouse River

Little Ouse River

Ling Belt

Toll

Forest Drive

Flint Pits

Lingheath Farm

High Lodge
Forest Centre

Brandon

Scale:

0.5 Km   1 Km

Information from Forest Enterprise, Tel. 01842–810271.

Grimes Graves. (English Heritage) a 7 km or 4.5 mile round trip on forest paths from Santon Downham. GR 818898. Prehistoric flint mines, 4000 years old. Set in area of open heath with lots of spring and summer flowers. One pit open to visitors all year — part time in winter. History of flint mining display. Tel. 01842–810656.

Brandon Heritage Centre. George Street. History of flint mining, rabbit and fur industry, forestry and other local history. Open weekends April to October plus Thursdays in summer holidays. Tel. 01842–813707.

Wangford Warren Nature Reserve — details page 46.

WALK: From the car park head down to the river and cross the bridge.

1. Almost immediately turn right down the steps and along the grassy river bank.

2. Cross the footbridge opposite St Helens picnic site and continue straight ahead to a waymarked post and turn left. At the next ride turn right (post 20) up the rise; turn right at the next ride.

Serried ranks of pine plus the odd silver birch and oak, some heather and broom growing along the edge of the ride.

3. At a T junction turn left (32 on tree) and at the road go straight across.

4. At the next broad ride turn left a few yards and then right. At the next intersection turn left and follow the track down to the road. Cross the road, slightly to the right, the track continues on the other side, alongside crop fields to the left and woodland on the right (Ling Belt). At the end of the fields continue ahead between the trees and at the

FIRECREST

next junction turn right. (If you wish to visit High Lodge continue straight ahead.)

5. At the road, Forest Drive, turn right and continue along to the end. It is a toll road in summer and very quiet.

A little distance to the left is Lingheath Farm, site of the Brandon flint mines — or pits to be more precise.

Cross straight over the Brandon – Thetford road and follow the ride ahead then left and right to the Santon Downham road.

6. Turn left for about 25 yards then right into another ride; continue as far as it goes then turn right. (If you want to visit Brandon turn left here and follow the path into town.)

Scrubby woodland on the left leads down to the river. On the right there has been large clearance of the pine plantations.

Follow this path for about half a mile till it bears round to the right and cuts across a very broad, very sandy track.

7. Turn left on to this track and follow it back to the Forestry Office car park. If you wish to see the village green take a right turn off the track; this brings you out on the road by some houses. Turn left and cross the green to the church; turn left down the avenue to the car park.

3. CAVENHAM HEATH, ICKLINGHAM, WEST STOW

CAVENHAM HEATH

Easy walk on mainly sandy or grassy tracks. Typical modern Breckland scenery, a mixture of wood, heath, river meadows and farmland. Takes in Cavenham Nature Reserve and West Stow Country Park.

Distance: 15km (9.5 miles). Two short walks 7km (4.5 miles) and 4km (2.5 miles). Extension via Tuddenham 19km (12 miles).

Map: Pathfinder 962.

Start: Ramparts Field car park. Off All01. GR 789716.

Buses: Bury to Icklingham service, via West Stow Country Park.

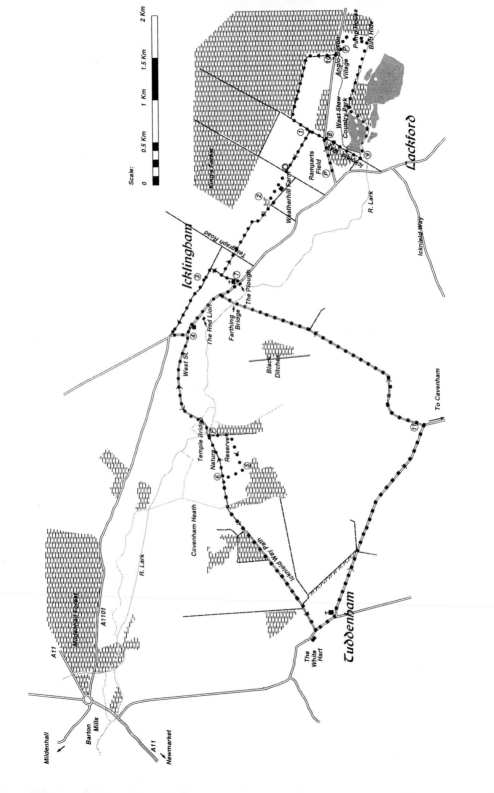

Eastern Counties. Tel. 01284–766171.

WHERE TO EAT
Icklingham, The Red Lion, Tel. 01638–717802.
Icklingham, The Plough, Tel. 01638–711770.
Both very pleasant; good menus including vegetarian choices.
Tuddenham, The White Hart, Tel. 01638–713061. Food, Wednesday and Sunday only.

LOCAL INTEREST
Cavenham Heath National Nature Reserve. (English Nature). Open heath; grass, ling heather, birch wood. 60 species of breeding bird; rarities include stone curlew, woodlark. Adders and lizards. Many invertebrates, small mammals and roe deer. Plants include vipers bugloss, dark mullein, mignonette, maiden pink, petty whin and suffocated clover.
West Stow Country Park. Most attractive site with variety of habitats — river, lakes from old gravel workings, wet woodland, dry birch and oak woods, heath. Reconstruction Anglo-Saxon village with small farm. Special events from time to time. Open all year 10am – 5pm. Picnic areas, toilets and Visitor Centre. Tel. 01284–728718.
Lackford Wildfowl Reserve. (SWT) GR 800708. SSSI created from worked out gravel pits by River Lark. Information leaflets at entrance. One of the best places in Suffolk for kingfishers, butterflies and dragonflies.

WALK: Turn left out of car park towards a cottage behind a line of trees. Turn left here on to a broad track, sign posted both Icknield Way and Lark Valley Path.

1. When you reach a row of Scots pines to your left turn left alongside them.

At the end of this field to your right is a big sandy bank with hawthorn growing on it; a disused pit. In the distance are the conifers of the Kings Forest.

At the junction with a farm track coming from your left continue straight ahead.

In this field are two dips filled with Scots pine — very likely disused marl pits.

2. At the end of the field turn left, then right on to a broad track which sweeps to the left; leave it and continue straight ahead up the side of the next field and down to Telegraph Road, a sandy lane. Cross the stile and continue ahead to a T junction of tracks in front of a flint wall. Turn right between the trees for a short distance then turn left.

3. Keeping the village on your left and arable fields on your right, follow this path to the far end of the village. At the busy road turn left for a very short distance.

4. Turn sharp right in front of the flint-built community centre into West Street; past the houses the road narrows and becomes a gravelly track over pasture land alongside the River Lark. Cross the river by the steep little Temple bridge.

So called because the Knights Temporal maintained it as a toll bridge on the London to Norwich road — on which you are now standing — in the Middle Ages.

Turn left across the car park and over the stile into Cavenhan Heath Reserve. Go straight ahead, then turn right through the heather towards the birch woods.

Most of Breckland must have looked like the landscape round here in past times. An abundance of mosses and lichens alternate with short rabbit-cropped grass. Attempts to reseed heather five years ago — the stripy patch on your right — failed. Heather needs moisture to germinate and get established and the weather has been too dry. To the left are sand and gravel extraction works. The sand and gravel seam runs across the heath and extraction will come right up to the boundary in the next few years.

5. The path enters the wood and turns right.

6. At the stile turn right on to the very sandy lane and walk back into Icklingham along the village street.

7. Take the footpath up the far side of the flint built, thatched All Saints church and turn right on to the Icknield Way Path and retrace your steps as far as the cottage on the road from Ramparts Field to West Stow.

8. Instead of returning to the car park, cross the road and take the path straight ahead which will lead you into West Stow Country Park.

9. Turn left into the park and right on to a path that will take you along the lake and the river. Past the Anglo-Saxon village and the Visitor Centre, you come to a bird hide looking over Lackford Wildfowl Reserve. You have a choice of tracks back to the main entrance of the park (where there is a bus stop). Turn right out of the park.

10. Take the footpath to the left, just past the cottages; follow it along the edge of the wood back to the Icknield Way Path where you turn left and, at the road, right back to Rampart Fields.

ALTERNATIVE WALKS. If you don't mind walking along quiet roads for about 4 km, through attractive and varied scenery, you can extend the main walk by turning left at (**6**) on the track across heath and woodland to Tuddenham village green. Turn left along the road towards Cavenham.

11. After about half a kilometre take the lane to the left which leads back to Icklingham, passing the Black Ditches away to the left (they can't be seen from the road unfortunately) to enter the village at Farthing Bridge. 19km (12 miles).

SHORT WALKS: 7 km (4.5 miles) Park at Cavenham Heath GR 758728. Walk round the heath and into Icklingham and through the village. Take the footpath by All Saints church (**7**); turn left at the top and along the path behind the village (**3**) to the Mildenhall Road. Turn left then sharp right (**4**) into West Street and back to the car park on the heath.

4 km (2.5 miles). Park at Ramparts Field. Turn left out of the car park towards the Lark Valley Path and turn right, left into the Country Park; right outside the main entrance, left at the cottages; (**10**) along the outside of the wood back to the Icknield Way Path; right at the road and back to the car park.

4. PAKENHAM AND IXWORTH

Well waymarked walk on the level. Country lanes, woods, fields and fen meadow. Water mill and windmill, both working. 6 stiles.

Distance: 16km (10 miles). From Thurston station, 2 miles return.

Map: Pathfinder 984 and 963.

Start: Park Pakenham Church car park GR 930671 or Ixworth Village Hall. GR 933703.

Buses: from Bury. Eastern Counties Tel. 01284–766171.

Train: Ipswich — Bury line stops Thurston station.

WHERE TO EAT
Pakenham, The Fox. Small friendly pub with reasonably priced bar meals. Speciality is 'huffers', gigantic baps with various fillings. Sundays set roast lunch only. Tel. 01359–230347.
Ixworth, The Pykkerell, 15th C. coaching inn. Stone flags, library with rugs, lots of woodwork. Country wines and good menu. Tel. 01359–230398.
The Greyhound, closed Sunday lunchtime. Tel. 01359–230887.
Fish and Chip shop, Tel. 01359–230966.

LOCAL INTEREST
Pakenham Water Mill. 18C. working mill on site of mill recorded in Domesday. Open: Easter – end September, Wednesdays, weekends and Bank Holidays 2–5.30pm. Souvenir shop; ice creams and soft drinks. Picnic site and childrens play area. Toilets. Guided tours, demonstrations. Tel. Hon. Curator 01359–270570.
Pakenham Windmill. Five-storey tower mill circa 1816. Restored 1950s. View by appointment.

WALK: From Thurston Station. Turn right up Station Hill; at bend turn right between metal railings on to a paved footpath alongside the new village green. Turn left into Sandpit Lane and straight over

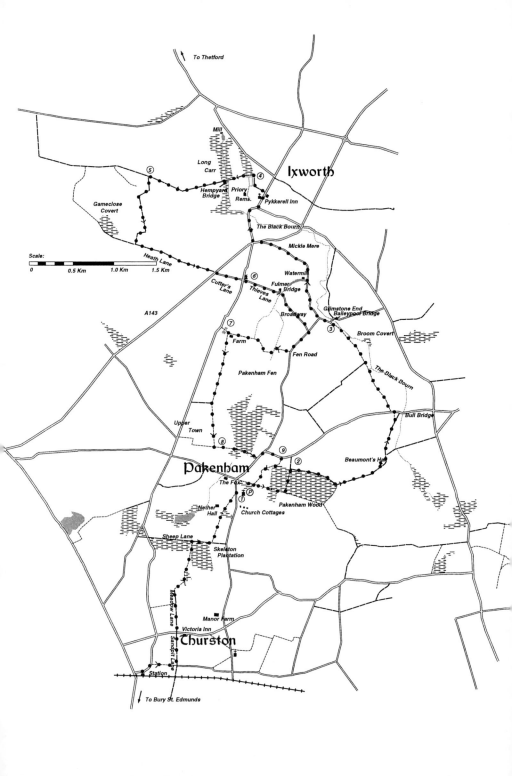

To Thetford

Mill

Long Carr

Ixworth

⑤

④

Hempyard Bridge

Priory Rems.

Pykkerell Inn

Gameclose Covert

The Black Bourn

Mickle Mere

Scale:
0   0.5 Km   1.0 Km   1.5 Km

Heath Lane

Watermill

Cutter's Lane

⑥

Thieves Lane

Fulmer Bridge

A143

Broadway

Glimstone End
Baileypool Bridge

③

Broom Covert

⑦

Farm

Fen Road

The Black Bourn

Pakenham Fen

Upper Town

Bull Bridge

⑧

Pakenham

⑨

②

Beaumont's Hall

The Fox

Ⓟ

①

Pakenham Wood

Nether Hall

Church Cottages

Sheep Lane

Skeleton Plantation

Meadow Lane

Manor Farm

Victoria Inn

Thurston

Sandpit Lane

Station

To Bury St. Edmunds

THE BLACK BOURN FROM HEMPYARD BRIDGE

the junction into Meadow Lane (Victoria pub on the right). When lane peters out follow the track between tall hedges.

Cross footbridge over ditch on the right then diagonally across the crop field into the trees on the left. Through the wood bear right and after crossing 2 stiles you come to Sheep Lane, nearly opposite the gateway to Nether Hall. Turn right and at a footpath sign to the left go through two kissing gates, across the parkland, coming out opposite St. Mary's church.

1. Go into the churchyard, cross the car park (where you will have parked if you came by car and are starting the walk from Pakenham) and exit by the kissing gate; walk down hill, cross the stile and turn right, into the wood and out again. After about 50 yards turn left into the wood again.

2. At the far side of the wood turn right along a very broad track and follow it as it bears left towards some farm buildings (Beaumont's Hall). Yellow arrows lead you past the buildings and up to the road. Cross straight over into the next field and over 3 stiles.

3. At a lane and a small grass triangle at Grimstone End bear right; pass the water mill on the left; Micklemere, fen and water-meadows to the right behind the houses. At the main road cross over and take the road ahead into Ixworth High Street passing Tollgate Cottage and a number of old timber-framed houses, some dating from the 14th century. Notice the pargeting on Dover House. At the church turn left and follow the footpath round to the right; turn left into the road at the bottom.

4. On your left is a spinney with banks thought to have been fish-ponds belonging to the Augustinian priory. Turn left through a gate between an avenue of trees.

Over to the left is Ixworth Abbey, founded in 1170 but the present facade is 17th and 18th century. Notice how the trees have all been evenly browsed at the same height by cattle.

Cross Hempyard Bridge over the Black Bourn and keep following the footpath signs past the wood and up the slope into open country.

5. Shortly after the path levels out take a track to the left which turns sharp right towards a pair of copper beeches. At a T junction turn left between orchards (Heath Lane). At the busy A143 cross over into Cutters Lane.

6. Where Cutter's Lane becomes Thieves Lane, the road leading north, to the junction with the A143, is the course of a Roman road and beneath the fields lie the remains of a 7 acre Roman fort, built around AD61, excavated 1988.

Pass the windmill and continue over Fulmer Bridge and along Broadway. Turn right along Fen Road for about 200 yards and take a footpath to the right across the fen meadows, crossing 3 stiles.

Many flowers in early July, including common and marsh orchids. Ixworth used to be rich in hedges. The one along the south side of Broadway, containing hawthorn, bramble, dog rose, elm, ash and hazel may have been typical.

7. On reaching a farm track turn left through the farmyard till you come to a signpost to the left leading you past a pond and into a field with mullein and wild hops growing in the ditch.

Towards the end of this path, around Upper Town, is an area which was very wet, full of rushes, reeds, mallows, mead-

owsweet, hemp mint and willow. In the 1970s it was under-drained and re-seeded. The ditching machine turned up hand made perforated clay pipes on top of flat tiles about 18 inches below ground. These drains must have been laid about 100 years previously. Water from numerous springs rushed into the ditch-es. The land dried up producing rich black soil and cattle thrived on the meadow grasses until the end of the 1970s when the gov-ernment offered inducements to dairy farmers to reduce the milk lake.

8. Cross a stile in the hedge on the outskirts of the village and turn left, past the back gardens, over the parking area and into the wood.

Wood contains cherry, rowan and field maple. The marshy end of Pakenham Fen contains yellow iris and Himalayan balsam.

At the road turn left and follow it round to the right.

9. After about 100 yards, past the Rambling House Hotel, take a broad track to the right towards Pakenham Wood. Follow the foot-path signs to the left, turn right across the fields towards the church and over the stile at signpost 8. Retrace your steps up to the churchyard car park, and on to Thurston if going by train.

There used to be a cattle pen at Thurston station when cattle were brought by train from Ayrshire, the last ones arrived in 1953.

THE WOODLAND
(CENTRAL SUFFOLK)

This area was so named, around AD1600, because its hard-to-cultivate heavy boulder clay soil retained its oak woodlands long after the lighter soils of the Sandlings and the Breckland. However by Tudor times the woodlands had largely become wood pasture —farmland trees. It is the central two thirds of the county, stretching from Haverhill in the south-west to Beccles in the north-east, down to the border with Essex along the Stour valley. It is now a land of cornfields, some vast prairies, but it is by no means a homogeneous landscape as it changes subtly and quite frequently. The highest ground in the county, over 400ft, lies south-west of Bury, around Depden. Here is rolling countryside with large arable fields, occasional woods, small remote villages. Further to the west in the more folded country around Lidgate and Dalham the chalklands start, running up to Newmarket and so on into the Breckland

HIGH SUFFOLK
CORNFIELD

where chalk becomes interspersed with, and then gives way to, sand. From here eastward and to the north of Bury the land is for the most part very open and generally flat. Between Eye, Debenham, Dennington and Stradbroke the soil is particularly impervious requiring great drainage ditches around the level and comparatively hedgeless fields. As long ago as the mid 1890s almost all arable fields in the clayland were under-drained. Trenches were dug all across the fields at regular intervals, using long narrow spades, then tile drains laid; an improvement on the earlier brushwood drains. In the 1950s machine-laid plastic drains were introduced.

To the south of Bury prior to the last war there was bocage country, small fields and meadows with high thorn hedges. There is just the odd hint of this still in an area of large open arable fields.

Julian Tennyson described the west of Suffolk as "more civilized" than the east; more orderly and controlled and even then on the high plateau the fields were larger with fewer and smaller hedges. Round the edges of the plateau, streams and rivers carved little valleys, altering the appearance of the countryside very much for the better, in Tennyson's view. Just west of the A12 from about Halesworth down past Framlingham, Saxmundham and Woodbridge, Tennyson's rivers and streams exert their influence and the landscape becomes typically 'East Suffolk' with many small villages.

CHARACTERISTIC AREAS

There are distinct areas in the Woodland with their own particular characteristics. On the **Felixstowe** and **Shotley peninsulas** rich loamy soils overlie sands and gravels. Bordered by broad shallow river estuaries which lap the saltmarshes at high tide, the valley sides rise in gentle folds to good flat agricultural land. At low tides the rivers recede to their narrow dredged channels exposing vast mud flats, thronged in autumn and winter with wildfowl and waders, their melancholy cries rising into the crisp air.

The Stour valley also has rich loamy soils over sands and gravels, and along the Suffolk bank from East Bergholt westwards the rivers Box, Brett and Glem carve little valleys into the hinterland. The countryside is undulating, quite steeply in parts, and the fields, except where they were turned into airfields during the second world war, tend to be smaller and more irregular in shape. The area is full of old timbered and decorated towns and villages which flourished with the medieval cloth trade.

Chalk breaks out around Claydon amongst the river gravels of the **Gipping valley**. The Gipping became very industrialized from Ipswich to Stowmarket with the opening, in 1793, of the navigation and its regular barge traffic until the railway increasingly took its trade. It finally fell into disuse in 1922. Though still fairly industrial its middle stretch is lined with water meadows and lakes, formed from old gravel workings, providing a very pleasant recreational area. Old watermills stand on the river banks, at Baylham, Needham and Bosmere.

Along the **Waveney** and **Little Ouse valleys** in the north there are pockets of rare valley fen and heathland. Dairy farming was dominant and many small hemp fields were scattered amongst the pastures and meadows. The labour-intensive linen weaving industry was concentrated in the north and north-east of the county. Many small farmers combined farming with part time jobs in the weaving trades. Retting pits to soak the hemp fibres were dug in the clay soils of the wood pastures. The industry was flourishing in the 17th and early 18th centuries but declined later in the 18th century. The names hemp and hempyard still attach to fields and bridges in the area.

In the furthest north-eastern corner from around Beccles to Lowestoft and down through the Ilketshalls and South Elmhams there is a part of the landscape both ancient and remote. Sparsely populated, it stretches away to the ever-eroding coast at Covehithe and Benacre with their shingle-bound lagoons.

LAND SETTLEMENT AND FARMING

Roman to Medieval times. In Roman times and even earlier there were scattered farmsteads along the river valleys where the woodland had been cleared. Up to the time of the Norman Conquest a blend of woods and moorland — undrained clay common with coarse grass, rushes and thorn, providing common grazing — would have covered the area on the higher ground between the valleys. Although the clay was difficult to work at first, persistent cultivation produced productive land and the variability of the soil over quite short distances made it very suitable for small scale mixed farming: grain, cattle, pigs, sheep and hemp, and so small-holdings developed around commons and greens in late Saxon and early Medieval times. As the Middle Ages advanced numerous small fields edged with hedgerows containing trees spread across the area.

There were two types of early settlement; primary and secondary. Primary valley estates and hall-farms ranged in size from outsize cottage to stately home. Typically the hall would be isolated in the midst of a curved fenced estate with a track running through the middle. These settlements were relatively stable; by contrast the secondary green-side tenements (dependant land-holdings) sited well away from the hall, on the edge of the estate were liable to multiply and sub-divide in periods of growth and to be amalgamated or deserted in times of recession.

In the 13th century a growing population gave rise to a thriving market in land amongst the peasantry though their land-holdings were often very small and, if they were scattered tending them was time wasting and inefficient. Farmers often exchanged pieces of land to acquire more convenient holdings so piecemeal enclosure was common. Partible inheritance, where land was divided equally amongst male heirs, was common in Suffolk and resulted in a pattern of small blocks of land not always cultivated or grazed communally. All this produced a distinctive *ad hoc* pattern of landholding which was interspersed with planned regular holdings where large areas of wasteland had been divided up between manors and tenements in lieu of common rights. As the population declined again in late Medieval times, exacerbated by outbreaks of Black Death — bubonic plague — in the mid-14th century, there was considerable amalgamation and consolidation of land holdings. The Sandlings and the Woodland suffered particularly from desertion at this time and sometimes only one or two farms survived from ten or more. Peter Warner in 'Greens, Commons and Clayland Colonization' says "... the landscape of East Suffolk is littered with the wreckage of Medieval manorization." These deserted farms are characterized by small moats and most parishes contain two or three empty moated sites. Some still have the splendid timber framed houses which were built in the 16th and 17th centuries.

Up until around 1400, here, as in the rest of the country, agriculture had been largely subsistence peasant farming. Over the next 300 years it gradually became more of a commercial activity, dominated by landlords. New fodder crops were introduced enabling more livestock to be kept. They produced more manure so more arable land could be cultivated. The population was growing and, just like modern times, ways had to be found to feed a larger population, resulting in an increasing specialization in farming.

17th Century. By the 17th century many fields had been carved out of the surrounding woodlands to create pastures and farm fields which were commonly bordered by belts of trees about 1 rod (5.5 yards) wide and interspersed with woodland. These borders were probably, originally, the remains of the woodland cleared when the field was created and they, typically, occupied around 10 per cent of the farm land. Although it is not certain what their purpose was they were used for grazing and making hay. They acted as game coverts and as a nursery for pollards. They also made hedge and ditch maintenance easier, and were sometimes used as farm roadways. Up until about 1770 roads were usually neglected and in a foul state in winter. From the late 16th century a growing demand for arable land led to many of these borders being ploughed up. They were often studded with oak pollards hundreds of years old, all being removed in the early 1800s. Small plantations began to appear in their place, perhaps to provide game nurseries.

The 18th and 19th centuries saw a new wave of green-side development, often coinciding with the parliamentary enclosure of commons and the encouragement to lay land drains to 'improve' common land. In 1850 the tax was removed from bricks and pipes which encouraged their use in drains. What was known as convertible husbandry, alternative husbandry or ley farming became widespread in this period though it had been practised here and there from the 16th century. Some previously permanent pastures would be ploughed up for arable crops for a while and existing arable would be sown with grasses. After some years these would be swapped around. These short term grasslands were known as leys. Some fields were to remain permanent pasture and leases often stated which fields should never be ploughed. By 1850 farmland in High Suffolk was about 50/50 pasture and arable. Ley farming improved the quality, and so productivity, of both arable and pasture land.

SPECIAL FEATURES

Moats. If you study any Pathfinder maps of this part of the county you will notice an absolute rash of moats sprinkled across the countryside but particularly around the centre and north-east. There were even more at one time but many have been ploughed up or filled in. Some moated sites appear slightly raised, the houses being built on the clay dug from the ditches — the moats acting as drains. In others the moat seems to have taken the place of a boundary fence. The moats of some farmsteads were an extension of the green-side ditches that bordered the nearby common or green and separated the common pasture from private houses and arable land. Castles were always moated and some historians suggest that various lesser landowners moated their manors and monasteries more as a status symbol than anything else. Moats were certainly used to keep domestic animals in and wild animals out and they often doubled as fish ponds. Most moats enclosed sites of less than an acre and some of the smallest ones enclosed parsonages and free tenements. Where a farm was moated the barns and other farm buildings were usually just outside the moat or on subsidiary moats. Most moats date from the 13th century but later moats, such as the 15th century one at Helmingham Hall, have straight sided walls of brick or masonry. Not all ditches qualify as moats, though no one seems sure where to draw the line.

Greens. A typical Suffolk village, particularly in this central region, contains several hamlets, farmsteads and greens spread over a thousand or so acres with one church and these days, with luck, a shop and a pub. Within living memory such a village also supported a school, a Nonconformist chapel and a variety of trade and industry. There was no need for a car to acquire the necessities of life. These greens are common grazing lands which are still sometimes used for that purpose. They are crossed by roads and typically have houses around the edges fronting the green and backing on to fields behind. Much common land has been fenced or cultivated but what is left is a legacy of the Middle Ages or Saxon times. The village of Cockfield for example, is a collection of eight widely spread greens; Wortham has two, two miles from each other. Mellis has one of the most extensive greens in Suffolk, about a mile long and still unenclosed, with the London to Norwich railway running through it and old Suffolk homesteads round its borders. Chippenhall Green, nr Laxfield, now a SSSI, is an excellent example of what a typical green probably looked like. It has survived in an area once full of greens of which only the names remain, attached to areas of arable fields. Hussey, Silverleys and North Green — clearly a late parliamentary enclosure from its regular rectangular field pattern.

Buildings. The older buildings of the area are also characteristic, being made from local materials. There was once a prodigious amount of oak, so oak framed houses, half timbering and beautifully carved barge boards are common, as is wattle and daub, the plasterwork covering it offering good protection from the elements. The Romans introduced brick making and brick works were widespread. Crinkle-crankle walls are another feature of the area; one brick thick they are considered decorative but they also provide shelter and maximum exposure to the sun for more tender fruit and flowers.

NATURAL HISTORY

Meadows. The chalky boulder clay gives rise to fertile ground with seasonably wet soils. This provides both good corn growing land and excellent grassland conditions and very many of the traditional old flower rich meadows were 'improved' early on. They have been drained, fertilized and cut or grazed — even replanted with rye grass. Since 1939, 95 per cent of Suffolk's grassland has been improved. Nevertheless there are a number of mostly small, often less than 2 hectares, unimproved, species-rich meadows and pastures surviving, now mostly protected reserves. Species-rich meadows are those which have been managed traditionally for many years. They contain large amounts of such plants as birds foot trefoil, cowslip, knapweed, oxeye daisy, bulbous buttercup, glaucous sedge, green winged orchids, pepper saxifrage, adders tongue and a great variety of invertebrates which depend on the plants for their survival. Wink's Meadow at Metfield and Martins Meadow, Monewden are examples, containing 2 and 4 hectares respectively. Both contain fritillaries and a variety of orchids; Winks meadow has the only known frog orchids in Suffolk. The three meadows at Martins have never been sprayed, ploughed or drained and are surrounded by ancient mixed hedges, and in the autumn are bright with meadow saffron.

Trees such as ash, field maple, oak, some small-leaved lime and hornbeam all do well in these soils.

Ancient woods are the other particular feature of the area. Nightingales, long tailed tits and garden warblers thrive in the coppiced thickets. Woodpeckers, tawny owls, treecreepers and nuthatches are attracted to the mature timber trees. Aspen and wild cherry which attract hawfinches will be found in many of the woods, though aspen prefers waterlogged areas.

MEADOWLAND FRITILLARIES

The clearings and grassy rides often provide a habitat similar to species-rich grassland, harbouring butterflies, dragonflies, bees, hoverflies and damselflies which are attracted to plants such as herb Paris, nettleafed bellflower (seen in Priestly Wood) and spurge laurel, which need undisturbed soil to flourish. In Bradfield Woods there are around 370 species of plants recorded. Oxlips, rare outside Suffolk, are abundant there and in Bulls Wood. There are also ransoms, early purple orchids, water avens, wood spurge, betony, bluebells, wood anemones, yellow archangel, wood sedge, primrose, pignut and bugle.

Of the two dozen or so nature reserves in the High Suffolk clay-lands almost half are woodland, 8 of which are ancient woodland or contain fragments of ancient woodland. One shows evidence of ancient origins; another is a new woodland creation scheme on redundant farmland which included the creation of meadows, ponds, hedges and rides. Seven other sites are meadows, ancient, flower rich, wet and dry. The rest are pits or incorporate pits of some sort; chalk, gravel, sand and crag, open water with fen or wet meadow.

MEDIEVAL WOODBANK
WITH COPPICE

70

5. DALHAM,
GAZELEY AND DENHAM

Well used and sign posted paths. Good grassy tracks and quiet roads through orchards, woods and farmland, some undulating, some flat. From the quaint but untypical, of Suffolk, village of Dalham the path runs along the bank of the (dried up!) River Kennet.

Distance: 12.75 km (8 miles).

Map: Pathfinder 983 and 984.

Start: Park Dalham village hall. (GR 724617) or outside the Chequers pub, Gazeley GR 719641.

Buses: From Bury or Newmarket. Eastern Counties Tel. 01284–766171. Stagecoach Cambus from Newmarket. Wednesday, Friday and Saturday, am only. Tel. 01223–423554.

WHERE TO EAT
Dalham, Affleck Arms. Tel. 01638–500306. Tables in front on the river bank — very charming.
Gazeley, The Chequers. Sandwiches only — on request. Tel. 01638–750050.

LOCAL INTEREST
Moulton, 15th century packhorse bridge over (dry) River Kennet.
Rede Hall Farm Park, near Chedburgh. Working farm based on agricultural life of the 1930s to 50s. Rare breeds and Suffolk punches. Tea room. Open April–September, daily 10am–5.30pm. Tel. 01284–850695.

WALK: Turn right out of village hall and after about 25 yards follow FP sign to the left over footbridge (river must have been dry a long time, its bed is well vegetated!).

1. Turn right over the stile and follow the pleasant grassy path, with the Hawson Hills rising to the right.

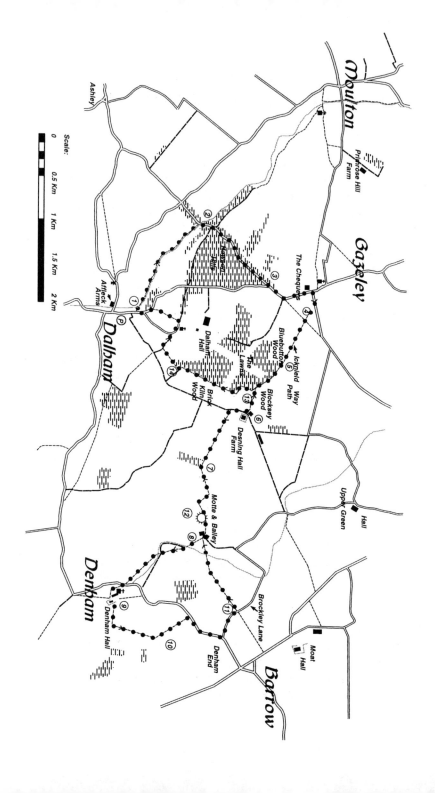

2. At the road turn right and take the path on the far side meandering beneath the beech trees, for most of its length. (If you are going to Moulton take the bridleway marked to the left.)

3. At the top of the hill are some playing fields, turn right down to the road, then left into Gazeley. Just past the pub turn right into Higham Road. Turn right on to the footpath through the housing estate built on a new village green.

NUTHATCH

4. Follow path (now called Icknield Way Path) between 2 houses, out of the estate and over a field to the left. Continue ahead through a landscape with wide open views of chequerboard fields of different hues.

5. At the end of the second field cross a footbridge and turn right into Bluebutton Wood. The path leaves the wood, runs alongside a field for a short distance then enters Blocksey Wood to the left.

6. At the next signpost turn left out of the wood and follow the path along the right of the field edge to and through Desning Hall Farm. Turn right along the road a few yards, then left on to the bridleway (blue arrow). Bit prairie-like up here with chalky, flinty soil.

7. Past a small wood turn left; cross the stile and take the path to the right, around 2 sides of this field. Continue to an orchard on the left with the overgrown earthworks of Denham Castle on the right. This is fenced off and the path follows the raised edge of, presumably, the old moat. Follow the footpath alongside the orchards to the cottages and through the gate.

8. Take the footpath to the right signed to Denham church — there may be herds of deer in the field. Go through a deer fence, turn right and follow this track to the Barrow to Denham road. Turn right then left up past the church.

9. The path goes into a field on the left — keep to the right of the field as the path runs alongside the impressive, but dry moat of Denham Hall.

The 16th century hall is now divided into apartments. The ivy-clad tower on the corner is a garden ornament.

After following 2 sides of the moat continue ahead to an orchard where you turn left and follow the broad grassy path.

10. As it curves round to the left it runs between high hedges to the right and orchards to the left. It joins the road to the right of a cottage where you turn right and, after about quarter of a mile, left into Brockley Lane.

11. Another ¼ mile, downhill, brings you to a footpath crossing the lane. Bear left across the field, up the next field and follow the path back through the deer fence to the cottages.

12. Retrace your steps to the left of the cottages, around the field, alongside the orchards, past the 'castle' and back to and through Desning Hall Farm, turning left over the footbridge into the wood again.

13. At the junction of paths, turn left — to your left is a typical wood boundary bank with coppiced trees and ditch.

14. Come out of the wood; turn right downhill, uphill, through another bit of wood. At the paved lane turn right towards the church.

Nice parkland around Dalham Hall with some imported trees, presumably ones fashionable when the park was made e.g.copper beech. Note the group of chestnuts on a very eroded bank with a great tangle of exposed roots.

Opposite the church turn left downhill between an avenue of venerable chestnuts. At the road turn left, past the unusual malt kiln to the village Hall.

Variation: Continue along the river to Moulton and from there follow the signs to Gazeley. Continue the walk as described via Denham, or cut it short at Blocksey Wood by turning right (**13**) and continuing through the wood instead of turning left out of it. Follow the path as described from (**14**). This walk is described in the SCC leaflet, length 6.5 miles or 10.5km.

6. FELSHAM — BRADFIELD WOODS

Easy, mostly well signposted paths; no stiles. This is cowslip country in April and May. Oxlips, bluebells, early purple orchids, violets in the woods, celandine and marsh marigolds on banks. Gently undulating countryside with views of distant woods and fields.

Distance: 15 km (9.5 miles). Short walk 8 km (5 miles).

Map: Pathfinder 1006.

Start: Park Felsham Village Hall GR 570947.

Buses: Limited service from Bury. Weekdays, Eastern Counties, Tel. 0128–766171. Saturdays only, Felix Taxis, Tel. 01787–310574. From Stowmarket, Wednesdays, Galloway Coaches, Tel. 01449–766323.

WHERE TO EAT
Felsham, Six Bells. Tel. 01449–736268.
Great Green, Plough and Fleece.
Thorpe Morieux, The Bull. Pleasant, friendly, plethora of plastic flowers. Good selection of bar meals with vegetarian choices. Tel. 01284–828320.

LOCAL INTEREST
Moats. There are eight 12th–13th century moats on the route and many others around — Moat Farm, Dakings Lane, just off Cockfield Road is a specially good example that may be worth a detour.
Ancient woodland. Monks Park and Felsham Hall Woods (known collectively as Bradfield Woods and managed by SWT). Thorpe, Felsham and Bulls Wood are all SSSIs. Bradfield Woods is one of the most outstanding ancient woods in the country, all its trees being native species, coppiced continuously since the Middle Ages when the woods were owned by the Abbey of Bury St Edmunds. The coppiced wood is still used in making tools, fencing, thatching and firewood. Over 370 species of plants have been recorded plus numerous interesting fungi, butterflies, birds and deer — the latter have to be controlled as they do considerable damage to the wood. Visitor Centre and explanatory leaflet available at entrance.

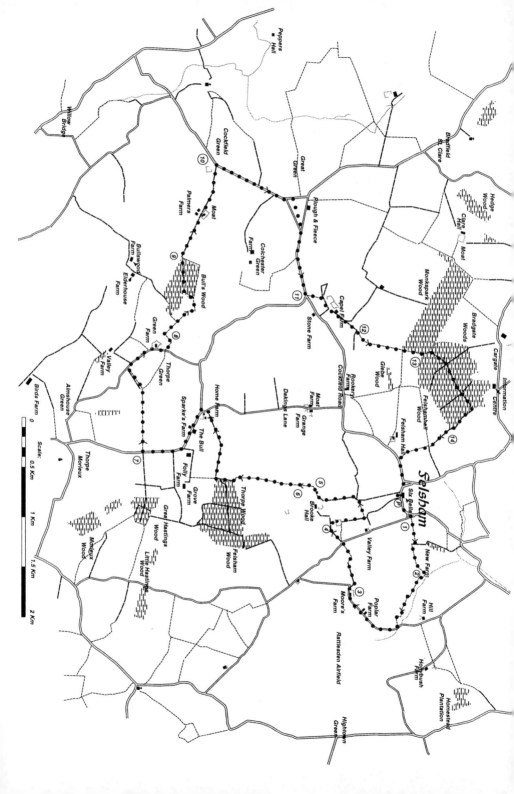

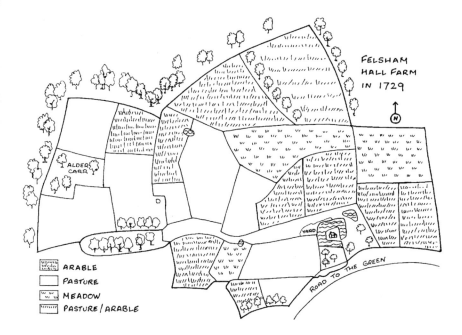

WALK: From Felsham village hall turn right along the road to a small triangular green.

1. Take the footpath on the far side, cross a small stream to a hedge, turn right and a few yards ahead turn left up a rise to the right of a ditch. Go down to a spinney and a footpath sign. Turn right and continue following the signs to the end of the field.

The fields round here are comparatively small, often with deep ditches and of varying heights. In the next field notice the small, older looking pastures behind the thick hawthorn hedge.

2. Turn right over the ditch. At the end of this field follow the signs into the next large field. When you come to the road turn right. (A couple of hundred yards up the road on the left is Hill Farm, a medieval house that has not been altered.) Follow the quiet lane past Poplar Farm; through the hedge to the left you may see a windsock on what was the old Rattlesden airfield.

3. At Moores Farm, which has the remains of a moat, turn right just past the moat, to the left of a thick hedge which has been nicely cut and coppiced. Go down the field to the left and at the bottom cut across the corner of the field on the right to a footpath sign. Cross the stream, mind the rather worn footbridge, and straight across the field ahead. Cross the road, slightly to your left and go up the wide gravelly driveway of Brooke Hall.

4. Turn right between 2 variegated poplar trees. As you pass a pond on your right turn left in front of the hedge behind which is the moat. Cross the ditch and follow the moat on your right round to the back of the cottage where, at some rusty railings, follow the footpath sign to the left keeping the hedge to your right. Towards the end of this field ignore a sign directing you diagonally across the corner (4a) and turn directly left across the field towards the footpath sign on the far side. The path is not clear. When you reach the sign turn left along the edge of the field — unfortunately, there is no alternative to going round 3 sides of this field.

5. The path veers slightly to the right towards a corrugated iron barn in the corner, bear right through the farmyard and then left at the sign. At the end of the hedge — lots of wild roses in it — cross the next field .

6. About three quarters of the way across you may see, certainly in the young green corn, a darker strip leading across to the far side of the field, showing where there has been a hedge that was grubbed out and/or a ditch that has been filled in with a different soil hence its different appearance. When the crop is ripe this strip may be a different height. Typical High Suffolk corn country round here with large fields.

At the end of the next field cross a ditch and turn left; at the end of this field cross another ditch into Thorpe Wood. Turn immediately right, following the track along the edge of the wood, to its end and cross a footbridge into the field where you turn right and follow the track around three fields to Home Farm. Bear left to the road and turn left to the Bull.

7. About a quarter of a mile after the pub, past a yellow fire hydrant, turn right on to a grassy track which curves round between an avenue of young trees. Continue past a modern bungalow with the remains of another moated site. Turn right at a T junction and carry on up the lane to Thorpe Green. Fork left, past a house called 'Oak Apples', into a field and turn left along its edge.

8. Pass a pond on the left and turn right alongside a newly planted hedge. Continue on this grassy track till you come to a hedge more or less blocking the way ahead, turn left, keeping this hedge to your right till you reach foot-path signs at the edge of Bulls Wood. Turn right and cross the ditch on your left into the wood.

Notice the ditch and bank which is a typical ancient woodland boundary, except this one is very straight and they are usually sinuous. This wood was a riot of oxlips in May. You can wander any of the rides of this wood.

OXLIPS

9. Turn right and follow the track to the far end of the wood. Leaving it to your right, strike out towards Palmers Farm which you can see across the very large field. Palmers Farm has a splen-did moat. Continue past it till you reach Cockfield Green — with a seat for the weary!

10. There is another moated site to the left of the green hidden in trees. Turn right at the road and follow it to Great Green. It can be fairly busy but there is a footpath. (The footpath between Colchester Green and Felsham Road is impassable.) Cross the green to the right to join the Felsham road which you walk along for about a quarter of a mile — marsh marigolds and celandine on the verge in season.

11. Past some white rails, cross a foot bridge into a field on your left. Cross the field diagonally, slightly to your right, towards a clump of trees. There is no sign of the path on the ground but you can just make out the footpath sign on the far side of the field. When you reach the trees the sign directs you ahead alongside a hawthorn hedge on the right. The double moat of Capel Farm is to the left. At the end of the tall cyprus hedge turn left — and pass the lovely

79

moated farmhouse, over a gravelled yard and on to a T junction.

12. Turn left up to the hedge; (actually the last vestiges of the original boundary of Monks Park Wood; 130 acres of it were lost to agriculture in 1970) turn right, with the trees to your left. Follow this path, which broadens out ahead, along the field, through some trees, along another field till you come to Bradfield Woods, where Monks Park and Felsham Hall woods join.

13. Just inside the wood is a hide overlooking Fishpond Lake. You can wander the rides of both woods as you like.

To continue the walk go straight ahead from the entrance of the wood to the first junction then turn right (blue arrow) and at the next cross roads (post 19) continue straight ahead till you come to the perimeter track and turn right.

14. Take a left turn out of the wood over a wooden bridge into a field. Go straight ahead past a pond, a ditch, and a belt of trees on the left. Turn right and then left and walk towards the houses. The footpath goes between the houses alongside a garden fence (Felsham Hall — with moat — is hidden in some trees to the right).

At the road turn left back into the village, passing the rather imposing church.

SHORT WALK. 8 km (5 miles). Start as above as far as (4a). Follow the diagonal path, through the hedge and continue ahead, bearing slightly to the left towards Felsham. You come to the road between the church and the shop and turn left towards Felsham Hall. Just past the entrance a footpath to the right takes you round the left of the house and across the field. Aim for the corner of Monks Park Wood if the path is not clear. When you reach the wood turn right, enter the wood and continue as from 13.

7. Gipping Valley
and Priestley Wood

Mostly easy walking on well marked tracks; a few field edge paths could be muddy in wet weather. The soil is chalky clay; the chalk has long been used for cement making and there are a number of pits around. The path meanders along the river, passing old gravel workings and it is hard to envisage that from the 1790s up to the beginning of this century the river was navigable up to Stowmarket. Barges transported coal, slate, timber, flour and various chemicals and the river was badly polluted by nearby industries.

Distance: 14.5 km (9 miles).

Map: Pathfinder 1007.

Start: Park in layby outside empty cottages on B113 near Baylham Mill Lane GR 110524.

Buses. From Ipswich, Bury and Stowmarket. Eastern Counties Tel. 01473–253734.

WHERE TO EAT
Gt. Blakenham, The Chequers. Tel. 01473–830455.
The Bell Inn, between Gt. Blakenham and Baylham. Tel. 01473–830349
Needham Market, several pubs and cafes.

LOCAL INTEREST
Needham Market, Alder Carr Farm, tea shop, shop, pick your own, and the best ice cream in Britain. Open weekends and bank holidays Easter to Christmas. Mid-June to Mid-September every day except Mondays. Tel. 01473–743078. PYO opening hours seasonal so Tel. 01449–720820
Baylham House Rare Breeds Farm, Mill Lane, Baylham. Located on part of the Roman settlement, Combretoviium. Great variety of animals. Visitor centre for information, gifts and refreshments. Open March–October 11–5. other times by arrangement. Tel. 01473–830264.

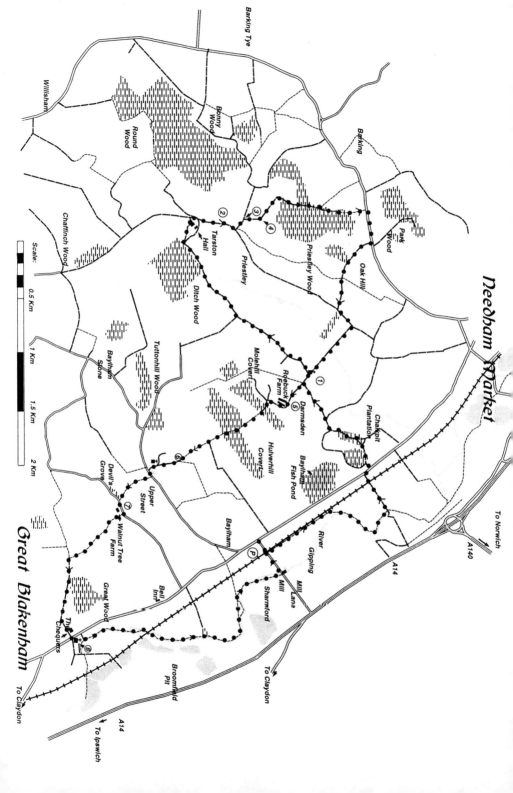

Priestly Wood, (Woodland Trust) was recorded in the Ely Coucher Book of 1251 but it was ancient then, having existed in prehistoric times. It lost its southern end to farming in the 19th century but the rest is unchanged since medieval times, enabling an amazing variety of plants to become established including nettle-leaved bellflower, broad-leaved helleborine, several orchids and primroses. Trees include small-leaved lime, hornbeam and wild pear, which is the most rare of native trees. The coppiced woodland contains maple, ash, hazel and seven varieties of elm. Nightingales common.

Bonny Wood, (SWT reserve). SSSI and one of the six ancient woods of Barking. GR 076520.

Blakenham Woodland Garden, Little Blakenham. Unusual trees and shrubs, bluebell woods. Open March–June (not Saturdays). Tel. 01473–830344

Stowmarket, Museum of East Anglian Life, open end of March to beginning November, Wednesday–Sunday and Bank Holidays 10.00–5.00. July and August every day. Tel. 01449–612229.

WALK: Cross into Mill Lane and turn left on to the footpath directly over the railway. After a while it turns right down to the river – yellow water lilies, Himalayan balsam. At a bridge over the river turn left and cross the railway once more, to the road. Turn right a short distance then take the footpath to the left and through the wood called Chalkpit Plantation:

The name denotes a modern wood on or near the site of a disused chalk pit.

Turn left on to a lane and follow it through Darmsden hamlet.

1. Bear left past the church and along this track round Tarston hall and continue on the paved track towards 'Priestley'.

2. At a junction of tracks head left towards a hedge and go through it.

3. A short way up the side of the next field cross the deep ditch to your right, where some trees run at right angles to it. Walk along the side of this field keeping the trees to your right.

4. Half way across the field faded white arrows on an oak tree in the ditch indicate a footpath to the left through the crop. Turn right when the path does, at the far side of the hedge, and continue straight ahead into Priestley Wood. Follow this track through the wood, ignoring a waymark to the left. At the road turn right for a short distance. Just past the white railings turn right, up Oak Hill, till you reach a small wood. Turn left and then right towards Darmsden church; bear slightly left then straight ahead at the next junction on a paved track to Roebuck Farm.

5. Walk through the farm yard, keeping to the left of the barns. Past a large Dutch barn turn right along a grassy path then left into some trees, down a slope and turn left. Continue on the broad track, across the field into Hulverhill Covert. Bear left and when the track divides into three take the centre grassy route. Continue ahead towards the houses in the distance. At the end of the field go left through the hedge, turn right towards the wall.

6. Go through a fence and follow the footpath to the hedge and up on to the drive. It becomes a lane, passes the church and flintstone school to the road. Cross to your left and take the footpath to the right, down a shady lane, along a field into Devils Grove, which rises steeply to the right.

There were badger sets along the left of this path which looked as if they had been dug out. A dead badger was seen on the main road nearby.

7. At the lane turn left and just past the pond with bulrushes turn right. At the side of a field go through a gate and straight across the field towards the cement works chimney. At a cross tracks (to visit the Bell Inn turn left here down to the road and turn left) continue ahead on the chalky bridleway. Turn left into Chalk Hill Lane which leads to the B113 at Great Blakenham, opposite the church. (The Chequers pub is on the left.) Cross the road into the church yard and follow the path out of the far side, down a grassy lane.

8. At the end of which you turn left down a very narrow alley between two buildings (with a FP sign engraved Gipping Valley Walk) and turn left along the river. Follow the river back to Mill Lane, turn left up to the road and left back to the layby.

8. Otley, Framsden and Helmingham

Predominantly modern arable landscape. Neat rectangular fields with straight, well kept mostly hawthorn, hedges with oak and ash standards. Odd bits of irregularity here and there. Drainage ditches very common, some very deep. Plenty of autumn colour. Not the easiest walk — many good grassy headland tracks but also poor paths with fields ploughed right under hedges. Very tall stiles into and out of Helmingham Park

Distance: 12 km (7.5 miles).

Map: Pathfinder 1008 and 1007.

Start: From the Otley to Cretingham Road branch left by the Baptist chapel. Park in lane near footpath sign. GR 208559.

Buses: Limited service from Ipswich. Ipswich Buses Tel. 01473–232600. Eastern National, Sundays only, Tel. 01206–571451. Eastern Counties Tel. 01473–253734.

WHERE TO EAT
Framsden, The Doberman. Very pleasant old inn. Garden. Varied menu with vegetarian choices. Tel. 01473–890461.
Otley, White Hart. Pleasant village pub, typical pub fare, well cooked. Vegetarian included. Tel. 01473–890312.

LOCAL INTEREST
Otley Hall. Moated timber-framed brick building. Open to the public at Spring and Summer bank holidays only but worth a visit. One of four notable Tudor houses in the area.
Helmingham Hall. 16th century with later facing. Very large; built round courtyard. Moat with working drawbridge. Hall not open to public. Deer Park. Gardens including superb walled garden open on Sunday afternoons May – September. Teas, farm shop. Highly recommended. Details from Estate Office, Tel. 01473–890363.
Fox Fritillary Meadow, off A1120. GR 188607. Open day, April/May when in bloom. Fritillary meadows are rare and need

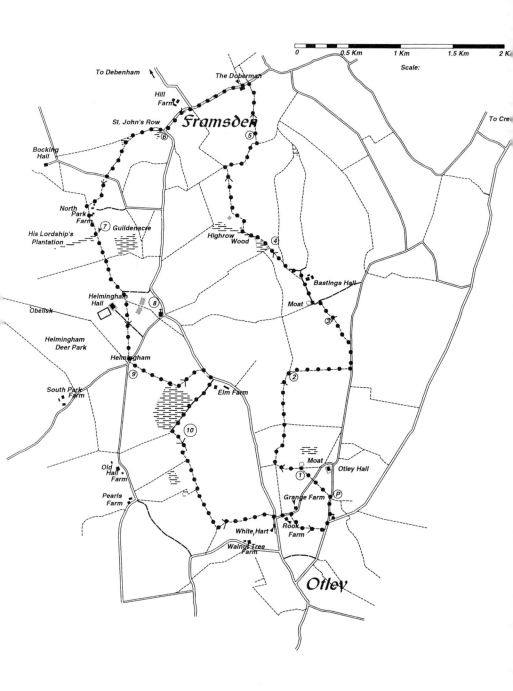

poorly-drained alkaline soil. Sheep graze meadow in summer to prevent grass smothering the flowers.

WALK: Footpath is about 200 yards from the chapel on the left. The broad headland path runs along the boundary of Otley Hall which can be glimpsed through the trees. Follow the waymark through the hedge and across the footbridge. Path lies diagonally to the left across the field to just before the wood starts.

1. Here a yellow waymark leads you over the ditch and along the right side of the field. Cross a footbridge with an oak to its left and turn right. At the end of the hedge leave the permissive path and bear right on the grassy track. Turn left into the next field ignoring a footpath sign to the right half way along.

2. At a junction, with footpaths to left and right (not ahead as on the map), turn right, go through the hedge, over a slippery footbridge and continue ahead along the edge of 3 fields. At the lane turn left for about 200 yards then fight your way through the hedge on the left, over the footbridge and aim diagonally towards the right hand end of the hedge opposite.

3. From this hedge aim towards another one leading across to the lane. (If you object to crossing crops or soggy plough, continue up the lane and turn left at the sign for Bastings Hall). Turn left and almost immediately the lane bends sharp right.

On the corner is an apparently intact moat with a thick growth of trees covering its platform.

Continue along the lane past Bastings Hall Farm and bear left along a concrete path beside a line of poplars. It becomes a stony track curving round to the left. Leave it here, going ahead and to the right between 2 hedges. Follow the path alongside the field with the hedge to your right.

4. At the end of the field cross the ditch into the next field, carry on round the edge of the wood, down the meadow entering the wood on a grassy track at the far end. You'll find a decaying footbridge to your right; don't trust it – scramble across the ditch and follow the meandering track to a T junction where you turn right to the field; turn left across its corner and right down its length, along the bottom and into the next field.

HELMINGHAM HALL

5. Turn right, then left and follow the hedge down this field to the road by the pub. Turn left through the village, past the Debenham Road and the pump. Cross the road on to the footpath going up the right side of number 100 St. Johns Row.

6. Just past the cottage garden, clamber down a ditch and through the spinney to the field. (the ill-kept, unmarked path goes between the back of the gardens and the spinney). Keep straight ahead with the spinney on the right. At the end of the field the path goes into the spinney and disappears amongst the undergrowth – don't follow it. A few yards further down the field, cross the footbridge and continue along the edge of the spinney, crossing into a newly planted bit when you can. Turn left, go through the hedge, along the side of the field ahead, down to New Road. Turn right and almost immediately left on to the footpath down the left side of the field; cross a footbridge into the next field to the left; continue ahead. Cross the drive of North Park farm, over a dilapidated footbridge and around the right hand edge of the field to the far side.

7. Climb the very high stile over the deer fence into Helmingham Deer Park. Cross towards the bridge over the stream.

The stream was completely dry; the sides very eroded. Some venerable old oaks in the park, including one that Constable painted.

Cross a stile into a paddock and out through a wire gate at the far end.

8. If visiting the church aim at the stone parapets between 2 ponds. Otherwise aim slightly left towards the far corner of the park, across the main driveway. Leave the park over 2 stiles near the road junction. Cross the road to the footpath behind the thatched bus shelter.

9. Cross the stile and skirt the paddock rail to the left. Turn right across some pastureland towards the corner of the wood. Enter the wood and, shortly, exit again to the left. Carry straight on down to Otley Road, turn right and take the next track to the right, back towards the wood; turn left along its edge and left at the end.

10. Pass a new plantation of oak and ash, cross a footbridge and round to the right to a signpost. Continue ahead under the power lines. Follow the footpath sign to the right a short distance then cross the ditch to the left. Before reaching the main road turn left at a footpath sign, along the right of the hedge and all round the field, a deep sinuous ditch to your left. Turn left to the road, on a broad track to the right of a tiny thatched cottage. Cross straight over and down the drive of Grange Farm. Just past Rook Farm follow the track to the right across a grassy field and out on to Cretingham road, turn left and into Hall Lane.

9. Framlingham, Great Glemham and Rendham

An easy walk mainly on broad well-marked tracks. The Glemham, Sweffling area is very pretty undulating farm land, well established hedges, smallish fields and pastures in the Alde valley. By contrast the Framlingham end of the walk has large fields open to the sky; a feeling of being in High Suffolk. Best perhaps when the corn is ripe. To be avoided when the oilseed rape is in flower if you are allergic to it. Eleven easy stiles.

Distance: Full route 20.75 km (13 miles). Gt. Glemham — Rendham 9.5 km (6 miles). Framlingham — Gt. Glemham 12 km (7.5 miles).

Map: Pathfinder 986.

Start: Car parks in Framlingham or by the roadside at North Green GR 311623.

Buses: From Ipswich to Framlingham. Eastern Counties Tel. 01473–253734.

WHERE TO EAT
Rendham, White Horse. A welcoming real pub. Snacks, tea and coffee served 12–3pm every day. Garden. Open fire. Tel. 01728–663497.
Sweffling, White Horse Inn. (does B&B). Usual pub fare including a vegetarian choice. Garden. Closed Mondays, except for holiday times. Tel. 01728–663787.
Great Glemham, The Crown. Good range of usual pub fare including vegetarian choices. Log fire. Closed Mondays. Tel. 01728–663693.
Framlingham, several pubs and at least two tea shops.

LOCAL INTEREST
Framlingham Mere (managed by Suffolk Wildlife Trust) Freshwater mere, dug out around AD1190, with wet meadows.
Framlingham Castle (English Heritage). 12th century curtain wall and towers. Open April–September 10–6; October – March 10–4

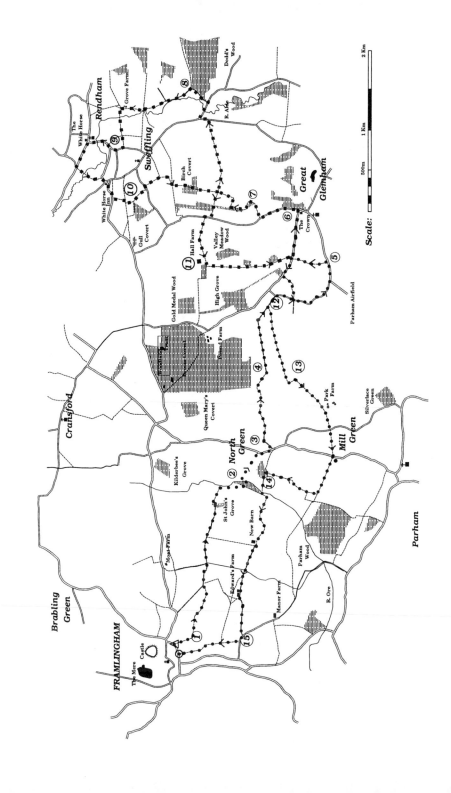

daily. Tel. 01728–724189.

Pound Farm Wood, newly planted woodland on disused farmland. Owned by the Woodland Trust.

Parham Airfield Memorial Museum in control tower of former USAAF—bomber base. Open March – October, Sundays and Bank Holiday Mondays. 11–6. Refreshments available.

WALK: Opposite Framlingham castle turn right into Castle Street and right again into Fore Street; take the bridleway to your left.

1. Leave it and continue straight ahead on a grassy track which curves to the right between fields. Pass a covert to your right, turn left to the end of the hedge and sharp right on to a broad grassy track. At the end turn right following the ditch on your left.

2. At a triangle of youngish trees bear left to the wood. Turn right then left on to a broad track through the woods. At the end, turn left and out into the field. Take the footpath straight ahead to a pink house, turn right and follow the road across North Green.

3. Turn left at a bridleway sign, passing a cottage and a pond. Turn right at the far side of the hedge and keep following the bridleway signs for about half a mile.

4. At a field end you come to a post and a tree both bearing faded white circular signs. Turn left, passing a tiny pond hidden in scrub, to your right and follow the broad sandy track. After passing a minor road to the left, continue ahead another half mile or so to a road, turn left for about 200 yards.

5. Opposite a red brick house take a footpath to the left, at another road turn right towards Gt. Glemham village.

6. Turn left into Chapel Lane, signposted to Sweffling. Leaving the houses behind, take a broad track to the right.

7. At the bottom of the field turn left, keeping the wood on your left. At the top of the rise turn right along the right side of a row of trees.

In the middle of the field to the right is a disused marl pit, colonized by trees and scrub.

At the end of this field cross the footbridge through the hedge and follow the path downhill, to the road. Turn left and a little way ahead, at the Sweffling village sign, turn sharply right. Cross the bridge over the Alde and take a broad track to the left between meadows and a wooded rise.

8. At the end of the wood the track bears to the left. When it turns right by some buildings go straight ahead into a field. Following the signs, cross five stiles and pass Grove farmhouse and its pond – is this the remains of a moat? Climb the stile on your left and cross the field, a footbridge over the river, then another two stiles, on to a grassy track with a new plantation on your right.

9. Go ahead through the gate, down a drive to the road and turn right. Follow the main road to the right into the village. Turn left in front of the pub; pass two roads to the right and take the footpath between two bungalows on the left. Cross a footbridge and a stile and keep straight ahead through the meadow; towards the end bear left to a gate in the corner. Turn right on to the road and follow it past the White Horse Inn, round the bend. Past a large solitary oak on the left there is a footpath sign hidden in the hedge. Turn left here down the side of the field. At the bottom cross a gulley and continue up the other side.

10. Cross the corner of this field and through a gap in the hedge. Turn left and carry on, keeping the hedge to your left. At the road turn left for a very short distance and take the footpath to your

OIL SEED RAPE
NEAR FRAMLINGHAM

right. Keep ahead with the shelter belt to your left. At the next field boundary go through the hedge and cross diagonally towards the trees on the far side. Follow the route over the footbridge up to the wood – Birch Covert. A faded arrow indicates the path through the wood, which is not clear, but keep heading in a SSW direction. At the southern boundary of the wood a clear path leads through the field ahead.

Notice the wood boundary – a ditch with hedge of blackthorn, hawthorn and boundary oaks. As it is a covert it would have been planted for game birds, probably some time in the 19th century.

Follow the path up the next field and turn right to the left of the hedge. Continue straight ahead to the road, turn right for a few yards, then left along an avenue of poplars.

11. Skirting Hall Farm you come to a signpost and turn left – unless you want to visit Pound Farm Wood – down a cindery track through an avenue of young trees. At the road turn right for a short distance, then left up to the lane and turn right.

12. You pass a turning to the right and a bit further on, opposite a cottage with wooden shutters, turn left up the right side of the field.

In the distance to the right you can see the new planting of Pound Farm Wood. Further on, over to the left is the control tower of the old Parham airfield.

After going straight ahead for about half a mile the track turns left, then right.

13. Pass between the buildings of Park Farm and follow the track down towards Mill Green. Ahead is a clump of trees hiding a pond; take the footpath just to its right, over the stile. Cross the field, another stile and footbridge, another field and you come to the road. Cross this and continue up the next field. Just before a sign to Parham Wood turn right on to a broad sandy track to Green Farm.

14. Turn down a stony bridleway to the left of the farmhouse. At the bottom turn left and then right around the field edge. By a large stag-headed oak turn right towards New Barn then left along a very well kept track through Edwards Farm.

15. At the road turn right for a few yards; take the footpath through the field to your right towards Framlingham. Keep straight ahead, then along a lane into the estate, down some steps and follow the green circular route signs, past the cemetery back into Framlingham centre.

The walk can be extended by following the footpath signs around the castle and/or the mere, which is a nature reserve.

To visit Pound Farm Wood. From Hall Farm (**11**) continue straight ahead, passing a pond on your left and a wood on your right. Follow the track round to the right then past the next field, round to the left and on down to the road. Turn left down to the entrance to Pound Farm on the right. Just to the right a footpath sign directs you up the side of a field with a ditch or stream on your left. At the end of the field bear left through the deer-proof gate into the wood. Retrace your tracks to Hall Farm and proceed towards Glemham as directed above.

10. FRESSINGFIELD TO LAXFIELD

A one-way walk taking in Chippenhall Green; return by bus from Laxfield. A circular walk is possible but means rather a lot of road walking. Several paths ill kept or ploughed right to the edge so you must teeter on the verge of drainage ditches. Several deep ditches need manoeuvring. Mainly treeless arable fields, but the area is interesting for evidence of the number of old greens.

Map: Pathfinder 965.

Distance: 8km (4.8 miles).

Start: Road by Fressingfield church. GR 262775.

Buses: Very limited service. Eastern Counties, Tel. 01473–253734. Riches Coaches run a usefully timed bus on Tuesdays. Ring them to make sure it will stop at Laxfield. Tel. 01379–388297.

WHERE TO EAT
Laxfield, Royal Oak. Comfortable local with big open fire. Till the mid-19th century farmers would meet here to buy and sell grain. Excellent bar meals, including vegetarian. Friendly landlord. Closed Monday lunchtime; open all day Friday and Saturday. Tel. 01986–798446.
Kings Head. Ancient inn, no bar, stone floors, wooden settles. Egon Ronay recommended. Tel. 01986–798395.
Fressingfield, Fox and Goose Inn. Occupies medieval guildhall. Known for its food. Tel. 01379–586247.
The Swan Inn, The Street. Tel 01379–586280.

LOCAL INTEREST
A number of old greens now all enclosed except Chippenhall Green. Silver Leys, Swan, Bayles and North Green on the edges of the walk; Husseys green, now all fields with a host of footpaths converging in the centre, an indication of antiquity.
Chippenhall Green, a large common on calcareous clay soil. Unimproved grassland with a variety of grasses and herbs including an outstanding number of green-winged orchids. Also cuckoo flower, cowslip, meadow saxifrage and marsh bedstraw. There are

boundary ditches and ponds which were used by cattle and horses traditionally grazed on the common. The farms round the edge hold common grazing rights which they now let out. This is a fascinating piece of ancient landscape to compare with the various areas of modern arable land that still hold the name of green. Chippenhall, a SSSI because of its meadow flora is managed by English Nature.

Fressingfield Guildhall, now a pub, and Laxfield Guildhall, now a museum of rural life, open on summer weekends. Parish guilds, as opposed to craft guilds had a religious and social role in the parish, with welfare overtones. Initially their activities took place in the churches. Guildhalls were built to cater for the parish 'socials' and so keep alcoholic refreshment out of the church. These half timbered guildhalls built in the early 16th century have decorative red brick work.

WALK: With the church to your left go downhill and turn right along the road, up Buckinghams Hill and take the right fork.

1. At Oak Farm turn right along the field adjacent to the driveway (no signpost). At the end scramble across the ditch and head diagonally across the field — aim for a free standing ash tree along the hedge.

2. The footpath crosses the ditch just to the left of the tree but there is barbed wire across it. Just to the right it is easier to cross and obviously people do so. A signpost by the ash tree directs you across the field to a clump of trees; follow the sign to the right, round the trees and a pond.

3. Cross a footbridge and continue ahead along Husseygreen Lane.

There was once a large common here with many paths converging on it. The lane must once have been a busy thoroughfare – notice the ditches on either side with hedges on both sides of each ditch. Most of the fields of Hussey Green are enormous but there a few odd shaped small ones.

Near the end of the hedges turn right across the field alongside a deep ditch.

4. Where three ditches converge turn left – you should be on the far side of the ditch but it means scrambling across, whether you cross now or later. As the ditch veers to the left cross to the right of the tree filled dip. Aim towards Common Hall Farm, ahead slightly to the left.

5. You reach a broad headland; follow it to the left round the field, then right towards the farm.

6. As the track leads into the farmyard, bear left along the field edge to a stile on to the green.

The walk continues to the right but if you have time do turn left and wander around the green, up to the old Roman road at the far end. There was once a windmill in the centre of the green.

Having turned right past Common Farm, cross the cattle grid and pass Rookery Farm.

It was formed from several deserted greenside tenements. The triangular piece at the eastern end of the green containing the words 'cattle grid' is one of these. The large post-medieval farmhouse is a typically partly moated greenside farm.

Go along the road till just past Laxfield Road and take the first footpath to the left. Follow this marked path, over several footbridges connecting the fields. The fields to the left here, part of Rookery Farm, are smaller and more attractive.

7. At Deadmans Lane, continue ahead over the ditch, which has no footbridge and the way round it is choked with brambles (bring your secateurs!). Continue on the marked paths along the drainage ditches to a corner where a sign points sharp left across a field.

8. Do not follow the line of the sign; take a more ll o'clockish route, you can just see the yellow mark on the post across the field. Cross a footbridge and aim towards Laxfield church in the distance. The fields around here are vast and hedgeless. Follow the path all the way to the road then turn right and almost immediately left in front of a leylandii hedge. Turn left then right at the next ditch. Follow the waymarks towards Laxfield ignoring any left turns.

9. Follow the path into a small wood – on your right is the Tank pond, built to provide water for locomotives of the Mid Suffolk Light Railway – cross the footbridge over the infant river Blyth and continue ahead to the village street where you turn left. Alternatively turn left before crossing the footbridge and walk into Laxfield along Gorams Mill Lane. The bus leaves from outside the Royal Oak.

11. THE SAINTS —
SOUTH ELMHAMS

Slightly undulating countryside that feels remote and timeless. Ancient water meadows still survive amongst modern arable fields. All Saints Common, mainly unenclosed and part of the ancient moorland is an interesting relic. The eleven parishes of the South Elmhams and Ilketshalls are known as the Saints. 8 stiles and 1 gate to climb.

Distance: 13.5km (8.5 miles).

Map: Pathfinder 945.

Start: Car park at South Elmham Hall. Here you can get a leaflet containing information about the area and suggestions for short walks.

Buses: Limited service. Waveney Community Bus Ltd. Tel. 01379–852568.

WHERE TO EAT
Rumburgh, Buck. Delightful country inn with cosy bar and quiet garden. Good home cooked food. Tel. 01986–785257.

LOCAL INTEREST
South Elmham Hall and Minster. Both on route. Impressive 13C moated hall, in medieval times the hunting lodge of the Bishops of Norwich who had a large deer park. The traditional East Anglian farm has a herd of British White cattle, an ancient native breed traditionally kept by religious orders or in parks. Information re. guided tours and bed and breakfast, Tel. 01986–782526. **The Minster** is somewhat enigmatic. The present ruin is thought to be an 11th century replacement for an earlier Saxon minster.
Metfield, Winks Meadow. (SWT and Plantlife.) Typical ancient meadow flora includes 5 species of orchid. GR 303798.

WALK: Follow the South Elmham Park farm trail to start with, over the footbridge, across the field and over the stile, then turn

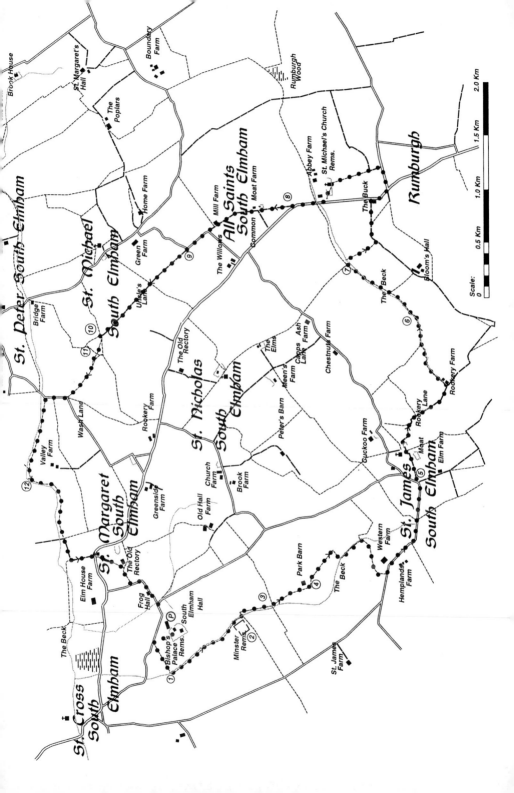

left. At the bottom of the slope, cross the footbridge.

1. Follow sign to left over stile into Countryside Stewardship Scheme meadows, three old water meadows with wonderful ancient hornbeam trees in hedges — hornbeam is a rare hedge tree — continue until you reach the minster.

2. Cross a stile to your right and the remains of the boundary ditch.

When the minster was built it would have stood on its mound, not surrounded by trees as it now is. It is made of great chunks of flint with sand and lime mortar.

Continue ahead with the minster on your right.

3. At the end of the next meadow cross a footbridge to the left. At the far side of the next field turn right at the hedge and with the pond on your left aim towards Park Barn at the far corner of the field. Go round to the right of the barn, cross the stile and turn right into a crop field towards the hedge in front.

4. Just past the pond on the left, cross into the next field, turn right and continue straight ahead.

Large fields with a patchwork of different coloured crops with few noticeable hedges in between. Before the last war the fields were usually small with high unkempt hedges.

Turn right over the ditch and follow the path, keeping the Beck to your left. When it goes underground turn right along the field edge, past the farmyard and left over footbridge and stile. Cross to a gate on the left; turn left into the lane along the village street. Notice a farm called Hemplands — a relic of the old linen industry.

5. Just past a road to the right, to 'The Farms', take the footpath on the right, beneath some trees, leading to and past St James church. At Rookery Lane, turn right and ignore the footpaths marked on the map to the left — they are solidly planted over. Carry on down the lane to just before the farm buildings. Turn left along the path in front of the hedge and ditch. This path follows the drain across vast acres of wheat from horizon to horizon with Rumburgh in the distance.

6. When you come to a patch of earth covered concrete, cross the drain and continue with it on your left. If you miss this crossing you may have to struggle through whatever crop is growing

ANCIENT HORNBEAM POLLARD · SOUTH ELMHAM.

right up to the stream.

7. After nearly a mile follow the field edge round to the right towards some barns. At the lane turn left and continue into Rumburgh. At the road turn right, pass the pub and take a left turn into Rumburgh Street. After about 100 yards turn left along the side of a field. At the far side take the footpath ahead through the crop towards a clump of trees, with an unusual church tower just visible. (No path had been left through this field). When you reach the trees bear left along the edge of the moat to the bridge which you cross and turn left through the churchyard to the road where you turn right.

The church, with its 13th century tower is all that remains of the Benedictine priory closed by Wolsey in 1528.

8. About 100 yards after crossing a bridge over the Beck, fork

103

right into a paved lane along All Saints Common. Parts of the common are still rush-infested rough grass which gets waterlogged in winter. Continue straight ahead across the common, past Mill Farm and along the lane till it swings sharply to the right.

9. The verge here is a nature reserve because of its rich boulder clay flora, including common broomrape.

Continue straight ahead on a pretty broad grassy track known as Uncles Lane. At a crop field follow the path through it to a small group of trees and a sign post. Veer left through the trees and continue ahead for some distance.

10. At the next group of trees, go through them between two ponds, turn left down the field edge towards some trees at the end. Great chunks of flint in the fields here.

11. Facing you are two yellow arrows on a conifer tree; follow the one to the right, to the right of the hedge and the very deep drainage ditch. At a bridge over the ditch cross into the field on the left and continue ahead.

The deep ditches contain water from the underdrained fields. It often runs clear and quite swiftly over a stony bottom.

At the road go right past white railings and ahead for about 100 metres. At the next bend take the path to the left.

12. At the end of the field veer towards the poplar plantation and bear round to the left — ditch to your left. A beautiful wide grassy track leads along the river all the way to the road where you continue straight ahead and round to the church. At the junction the footpath sign directs you across the churchyard, through a white gate, across a footbridge to cut across the corner of the field to a vestigial stile — 2 breeze blocks. Cross to another white gate in front of the Old Rectory, turn right then left into a lane. Continue past Frog Hall back to South Elmham Hall.

SHORTER WALKS. Follow the walks suggested in the South Elmham booklet — St Cross Farm Walks.

12. WORTHAM LING
TO REDGRAVE FEN

Pleasant walk through heathland, birch woods and along the infant river Waveney in Redgrave Fen. Much of the walk is through arable farm land where a few paths have not been well maintained. You may need to manoeuvre steep banks and ditches. 11 stiles.

Distance: 15 km (9.5 miles).

Map: Pathfinder 964.

Start: Car park at west end of Wortham Ling, just off Redgrave Road. GR 089797.

Buses: Limited service from Diss. Coach Services Ltd. Tel. 01842–752226. Waylands Minibus Services Tel. 01502 –716989.

WHERE TO EAT
Redgrave, The Cross Keys. Usual pub fare, very good fish and chips. Tables out front overlooking the quiet village street. Tel. 01379–898510.
Wortham village has a pub and a tea shop.

LOCAL INTEREST
Redgrave and Lopham Fen. (National Nature Reserve). RAMSAR site and SSSI; managed by Suffolk Wildlife Trust. The largest remaining area of valley fen in England, it includes sedgebeds, reedbeds, wet heaths, woodland and open water. The whole reserve is full of old peat pits, the old walkways between them now fen meadow. In the 1950s a pumping station was licensed to draw a million gallons of water daily from the chalk aquifer beneath the fen. As peat dries out it breaks down, releasing nutrients which change the flora and fauna. Accumulated scrub is being cleared, some going to Eye power station, some for garden mulch and some for charcoal. The area is grazed by a flock of Hebridean sheep, a small breed of cattle, similar to the Suffolk Red Poll and the Polish Konik ponies. The reserve contains a great variety of plants and animals that have become rare in the last quarter of a century. You

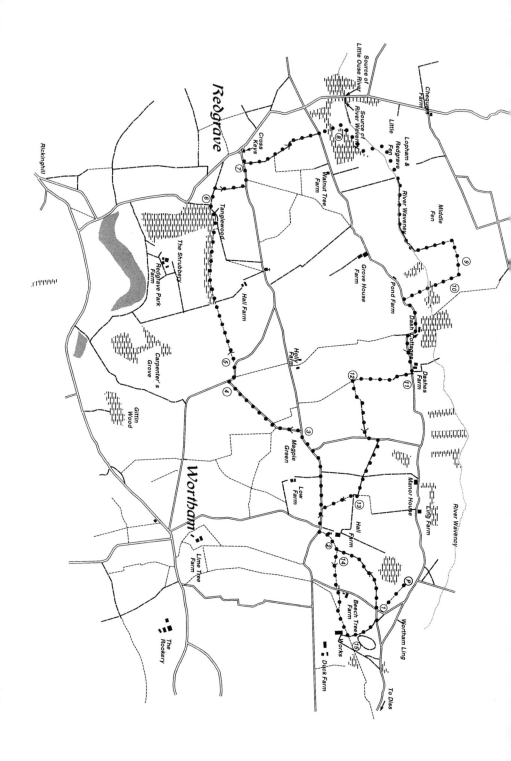

may see the very rare raft spider — brown and yellow striped and two inches long; also plenty of adders, but you will need to be very quiet to see them.

Wortham Ling, another SSSI (SWT) reserve. One of Wortham's two large commons, with rights to graze 200 sheep; nowadays only a few gypsy ponies graze. Mixture of heathland, short acid grassland, woodland, ponds and chalky areas. Butterflies abundant — small copper, small heath, gatekeeper, grayling and green hairstreak all present.

WALK: Facing the information board turn left across the heath. At the fork keep left and after about 100 yards take the right of 3 paths and keep straight ahead across a broad track to the road. Turn right up to a white thatched cottage.

1. Turn right on to the footpath and into a field; pass the garden of another cottage and cross a stile into a field, keeping to the left edge of the meadows all the way. To the right is a river with highland cattle beyond.

2. After several stiles the path crosses diagonally towards the church — in the middle of the field is yet another stile — go through a kissing gate into the pleasantly overgrown churchyard with some old yew trees and a vast round tower. At the road turn right towards Redgrave.

TARPAN   POLISH PONIES

3. After about half a mile turn left into the quiet Mellis road, through Magpie Green. Another half mile brings you to a broad sweep of grass with a road across it.

4. Turn right and down the dip. Climb a steep bank to your left to rejoin the path. A signpost hidden in the bank.

5. At the top turn left towards the trees and follow the path along the edge of the field.

Very Norfolk-like here — big fields and wide skies with that certain quality of light that seems peculiar to Norfolk.

At the end of the field continue ahead towards the wood, then alongside it. At some ramshackle barns the track veers away to the right, keep on straight ahead past the barns, the coppiced wood on your left. The path is uneven to start with but soon improves.

6. Follow round the end of the wood, cross the ditch and aim towards the houses then down the road. After a short distance turn right by a brick and flint wall on to the footpath across two fields to the road. Turn left into the village and the pub.

7. Alternatively, just before reaching the pub, turn right on to a broad track, cross a wide open prairie, down the side of a spinney to the road. Continue straight across on to the permissive path into the nature reserve.

8. You can wander through the reserve by a number of tracks and there is a plan at the entrance.

Look out for the Polish ponies. The Poles are trying to recreate the extinct Tarpan, a wild horse, ancestor to the modern domestic horse. It is a strong hardy little horse, acclimatized to the soggiest conditions. It can live on next to nothing and is very good natured. The plan is to breed a herd of 25 to keep down the growth on the wettest fen. They are most efficient and cheaper than mowers!

9. Aim for the far north east corner where you leave the reserve and take the footpath crossing the field ahead.

10. When it joins another path at right angles turn right and follow it across two footbridges, turning left at the road past a low white house. Round a bend you will see a collection of farm buildings on the left — The Dashes — and a new looking house opposite.

11. Turn right past this house on to a track which after a 100 metres crosses a ditch on the left into the next field.

12. At the top of this field turn left up the far side of the ditch towards sign saying 'No horses please'. (Be sure to keep the ditch on your left, it is exceedingly steep and difficult to cross at the top.) Follow round the next field to a very wide path between hedges and dilapidated sheds. At the road turn left for a short distance then right by some trees.

Across to your left is the lovely old Manor House surrounded by parkland. The soil around here is chalky sand with big lumps of flint.

At the next cross tracks continue ahead, then round the field to a corner where the track heads on downwards, with the church diagonally to the right.

13. This is not a right of way so you should head off into the crop towards the road — no sign post but the path was just discernable. Scramble down on to the road, turn left back through the churchyard and across the field diagonally.

14. At the far corner cross the stile to the right into a small plantation of young cherry trees. Go up a rise and through the crop then between two cottages, through the hedge and down the drive of one of them; there is a small pond on the left by the road. Veer left, over the stile to the right leading to a gate that is very difficult to open — you may have to climb it. Ahead is yet another stile into a grassy field. At the far end a stile to your left leads to a path marked diagonally through the crop towards a cream building and a hedge.

15. Passing this, you reach a road across the Ling. Keep to the left of this and work your way back across the Ling to the car park.

COMMON
COTTON GRASS

13. Long Melford to Glemsford

Generally well signposted tracks through farmland with open panoramic views of pleasantly undulating countryside. The village of Glemsford shows its industrial past and is not improved by considerable modern development. The two towns were important textile centres in the 15th and 16th centuries. Six stiles.

Distance: 14.5 km (9.24 miles) or 12 km (7.5 miles).

Map: Pathfinder 1029.

Start: Park near Long Melford Holy Trinity Church GR 867466.

Buses. From Sudbury, Felix Taxis. Tel. 01787–310574. Eastern Counties to Sudbury.

WHERE TO EAT
Glemsford, The Black Lion, Lion Street. Good pub fare. Tel. 01787–280684.
The Crown, Brook Street, Tel.01787–281111. **The Angel.** Tel. 017187–281671. **The Cherry Tree,** Tye Green. None of these three do food, but may make a sandwich.
Long Melford, various pubs. Cafes include: **Antique Cafe,** Foundry House, Hall St. Tel. 01787–378535 **Carousel Tea Rooms.** **White Hart,** Little St. Mary's Tel. 01787–311511 .
Stanstead, White Hart Inn, Lower St. Closed Mondays. Tel. 01787–280902.

LOCAL INTEREST
Kentwell Hall. Magnificent moated manor; Tudor. Rare Breeds farm, gardens and woodland walk. Private family home. Home-made lunches and teas. Opening times vary, Tel. 01787–310207 for details.
Melford Hall, another imposing Tudor manor. Part of the moat survives, the rest is a sunken garden. National Trust. Opening times vary, Tel. 01787–880286.
Glemsford, has several impressive Tudor houses built for wealthy wool merchants in the time of the 'Old Draperies'. The silk mill is early Victorian. Flax Lane is another reminder of Glemsford's long

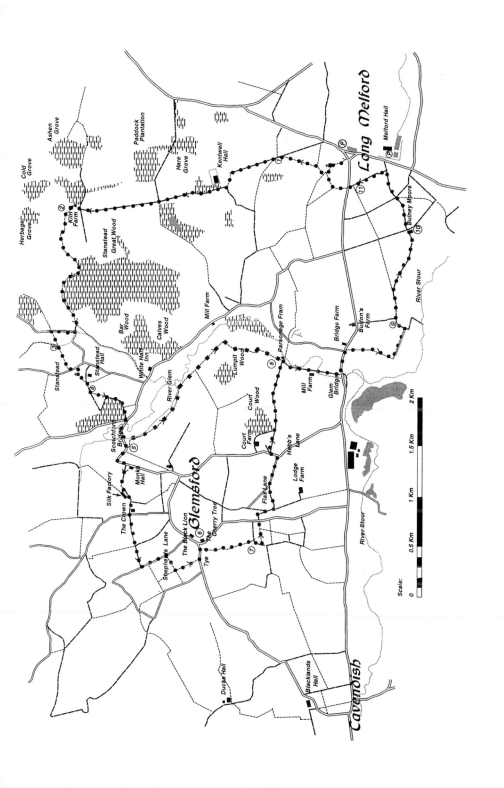

involvement with the textile industry.

Giffords Hall Farm, on the Stanstead to Hartest Road. Family home and smallholding with vineyards, winery, organic vegetable garden, wild flower meadows grazed by St. Kilda sheep. Farm shop and Tea Rooms. Open Easter – October daily 12 noon–6pm. Also do B & B Tel. 01284 –830464.

WALK: Follow the footpath round the left of the church then go straight ahead to the left of a paddock. Climb the stile into the paddock and cross diagonally to the right. Cross the next stile, through some trees, another stile then take the path rightish, aim half way up the lime avenue.

1. Turn left up the avenue and just before the gate to the hall follow the signs to the left. The path leads between arable fields on a high plateau. Continue between the buildings of Kiln Farm and round to the left.

2. At the field go left, following the line of the drain. When you reach the wood follow its boundary on your left.

There is a very deep ditch separating field and wood with a spring fed stream and large trees growing along the ditch.

Turn right at the road then left at the first footpath sign; climb the bank and cross the field more or less straight ahead to a stream with a signpost.

3. Cross the stream and head up over the next field, aiming slightly to the left towards a house with two dormer windows. (No signs of the paths on the ground but splendid new signposts!) At the road turn left, go through the church yard and down the field at the far side.

4. After a short distance the footpath cuts across the field to the corner of the wood — no sign of it on ground — and heads downhill towards the road. If you want the pub in Stanstead take the path to the left shortly before reaching the road, otherwise go down the steps to the road, turn right then fork left over the bridge over the Glem.

5. If you want to avoid Glemsford turn left at the corner after the bridge on to the path along the river valley to Parsonage farm, then follow from (8) in the longer walk. At Monks Hall — a pink medieval building — take the footpath up the right side of it and

MERCHANTS HOUSE · NOW BULL INN

follow it past the silk factory to the road (Crown pub on the left). Turn right and almost immediately left past house backs then alongside rough land with scrub and flowers. Continue straight ahead to Shepherds Lane where you turn left. Take the second footpath signed to the right, along the hedge, then turn left down to Tye Green.

6. Across the Tye from the Cherry Tree the footpath leads between two tall hedges to a field; cross towards the hedge straight in front of you, through a hole in it and to the right, round the playing fields. At the far side go down the lane on to the estate and follow the road round to the right.

7. Follow the footpath on the left to the road opposite the, disused Cock pub and to its left through its car park. At a wire fence, cross the stile and turn right; take the next footpath to the left, past the front of some houses; left over a footbridge and downhill to Flax Lane. Turn right to the main road (Hobbs Lane) turn left and take the footpath a few yards along to the right. Continue on this track to nearly Parsonage Farm.

8. Turn right (or continue straight ahead if you walked along the river path) on to a grassy, stony track. The Glem, a mere stream here, is to your left. Pass Mill Farm (once Glemsford Mill) over the river and down to the road where you turn left — very busy road, but only a short distance — to a footpath on your right. This green

113

lane leads to a field; go through the hedge to the left and follow it downhill to a chain link fence and turn left towards a gravel track.

9. Turn left past a black timber barn; a footpath branches off to the left over a field, the most direct route back to Long Melford. But continue on the concrete path to Bulney Moors, marked by a triangle of rough ground and the remains of some building.

10. Continue ahead nearly to the road, then turn left past two chestnut trees; continue to the next road.

11. Just before you get there the field path from near the black barn, joins the path. Cross the road and go over a bar in the wall, through a hole in the hedge and follow the signs over a stile, into a paddock. Cross the paddock to a stile on the far side and bear right across the field to the church.

14. Thorington Street, Polstead and Stoke by Nayland

RIVER BOX
RIFFLED STREAM

Lovely walk on well maintained paths in gentle hilly country; mainly through meadows, along the River Box and shaded country lanes. Few arable fields and the ever present landmark of Stoke by Nayland church tower. 13 stiles — several have a movable top bar for easier climbing.

Distance: 12.5 km (7.75 miles).

Map: Pathfinder 1053 and 1052.

Start: Thorington Hall GR 013354, park at roadside. Stoke by Nayland GR 988363.

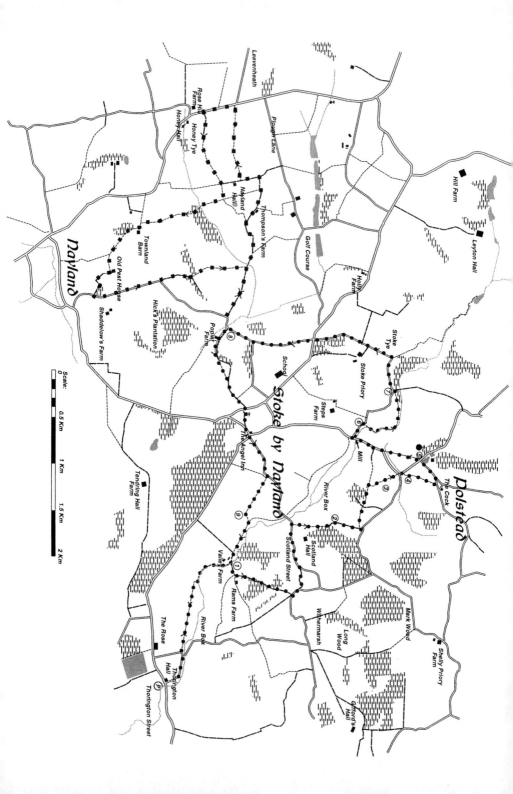

Buses: From Hadleigh. Wednesdays and Saturdays. Eastern Counties Tel. 01473–253734; From Harkstead, Hedingham and District Tel. 01787–460621, From Colchester, Carters Coach Services Tel. 01206–766962.

WHERE TO EAT
Polstead, The Cock. Old village pub with friendly and obliging landlord who will produce something to eat at any time if not too many customers. Open all day weekends. Tel. 01206–263150.
Stoke by Nayland, The Angel Inn. Rather smart with very good bar meals. Tel. 01206–263245. **The Crown,** Tel. 01206–262346, **The Black Horse,** specializes in curries. Closed Mondays. Tel. 01206–262504.
Thorington Street, The Rose, bar meals. Tuesday to Saturday. Sunday, roasts only. Closed Mondays. Tel. 01206–337243.
Nearest place for tea; **The Essex Rose, Dedham** or **Rose Hill Farm Tea Room, Leavenheath.** Open Easter to October, Friday – Sunday and Bank holidays.

LOCAL INTEREST
Stoke by Nayland. A wealth of timber-framed medieval buildings, notably the Guildhall and Maltings in School Street. Most impressive church at highest point of ridge between the Stour and Box valleys.

WALK: Down the lane past the mill and at the road turn left. The footpath is in front of you between two cottages; it leads round the meadow, through a hedge into a cultivated field with the river to your right. The official path follows a wide track through the crop and the stony soil can be very muddy. A waymark leads you into the next field where the sandy track follows the river.

Notice that the river here runs clear over a stony bed — unusual for Suffolk. When you get to Valley Farm you will see that, by the ford, the stream has been narrowed by the placement of large stones on either side, this causes the riffles and the clear oxygenated water. Compare it with the sluggish muddy water upstream of the footbridge.

1. Cross the bridge and continue a short way up the track to Rams Farm. Take the shady bridleway to the left; it brings you up to a lane where you turn left for a short distance. As the lane

117

FARMLAND AROUND
STOKE BY NAYLAND

swings to the right turn left on to a broad track, downhill, round two sides of the field. Arriving at Scotland Street turn left. At the bottom of the hill, just past Scotlands Farm, turn right over a footbridge and low stile. Follow the path through the meadow; near the end cross the stile on the right and follow the arrow to the left.

You cross a field of very short grazed grass with isolated thistles sticking out of it — good example of what an active rabbit colony can do.

2. At the far side of the field, over a stile, the path leads through some scrubby wood, mainly elder, to some steps up to another stile on to a broad stony track where you turn right up hill. Turn left through a kissing gate, follow the path to the stile, on to the lane and follow the sign post across the lane to your left. Cross the next stile and go right.

3. Cross the field diagonally under the power lines. Polstead church sits in a field over to the left. Cross the stile at the corner of the field into the road ahead (to Boxford). Just past the first house (Bells House) turn right on to the footpath to Polstead Green.

4. Cross another stile and continue ahead towards some houses, over another stile, past the end of the cul-de-sac and continue ahead to Polstead Green and The Cock Pub. With the pub at your back turn right over the village green down the pretty village

118

street. Pass a large pond on the right and cross the road into the field opposite.

5. Cross the field diagonally to the left and by a white lodge house turn right on to the road. After crossing the river turn right into Mill Lane.

6. Just after passing the lovely old red brick mill you cross a stile to the right and follow the river till you reach a stile on the right leading into a patch of willow carr. When you come into a crop field, follow the broad headland path round to the right through a kissing gate on to a lane.

7. Go more or less straight ahead, back on to Mill Lane — an extremely quiet lane, sunken for much of its length. Follow it all the way to the main road and down the far side, where it opens out for a while and you will see Stoke by Nayland school over to the left.

Very mixed vegetation; birch, chestnut, holm oak, oak, field maple, Scots pine, cherry, sweet chestnut and hawthorn.

On the left you pass a lane and a wood; continue ahead downhill to a T junction.

8. Follow the concrete track to the left by Poplar Farm, across the concrete hardstanding; continue ahead along the stony track to Stoke by Nayland church. Turn right and take the footpath alongside the church and into the village. Cross over by the Angel Hotel, and go down Scotland Street. After 200 yards the footpath goes to the right through the hedge and into a field. Turn left and follow the path down a steep hill, past a bramble thicket on the right with poplar trees beyond. It bears slightly left on a clear track through the crop.

9. Cross a low stile into the meadow, then another stile on to a track. Bear left towards Valley Farm again and retrace your steps, following the yellow arrows, through the meadows, crop field and another meadow. At Thorington village Street, bear left and just before the bridge turn right into the lane and back to the car.

Shorter walks: 8km (5 miles). From Stoke by Nayland, down Scotland Street to footpath over footbridge by Scotland Hall. Then as main walk to Polstead and back to Stoke by Nayland. 6 km (3.75 miles). Start as above, pass Polstead Mill, pass footpath on right and take next footpath on left passing Steps Farm; follow it to the road, turn left along road to Stoke by Nayland Church, then as 5 mile walk.

Longer walk: From the junction at Poplar Farm turn right to Thomson's Farm by an ancient green Lane. On to Leavenheath and back via Honey Tye, through orchards to Townland Barn, Old Pest House, up a lane with some very large pollards to Poplar Farm and continue as main walk.

(See leaflet published By Dedham Vale and Stour Valley Project. Suffolk County Council, Tel. 01473–585658.)

Leavenheath, Hare and Hounds. Tel. 01787–210473.

Rose Hill Farm Tea Room — see above.

15. Holbrook to Harkstead

Gently undulating country through meadows and arable fields on the Shotley peninsula; along the sandy shore of the River Stour with areas of saltmarsh and low crumbly cliffs where the teeth and bones of mammoth, bison and elephant have been found. Some parts are easy and well signposted. Too many are well signposted but without visible paths on the ground. Lovely views.

Distance: 12.5 km (8 miles).

Map: Pathfinder 1053 and 1054.

Start: Park in layby by lake in Fishponds Lane. GR 173362.

Buses: from Ipswich to Shotley pass through Holbrook and Harkstead. Eastern Counties. Tel. 01473–253734.

WHERE TO EAT

Harkstead, The Bakers Arms. Good home-cooked bar meals including vegetarian. Tel. 01473–328595.
Holbrook, The Compasses. Good varied menu, vegetarian included. Tel. 01473–328332.
The Tea Shop, next to village shop. Open Monday–Friday 8.30am–6.00pm. Weekends and Bank Holidays 10am– 6.00pm. Range of teas and coffees. Home made cakes and snacks. Childrens area with toys and high chair.

LOCAL INTEREST

Alton Water. Designated SSSI because of importance for breeding and wintering birds. Reservoir created in the mid 1970s to provide water to Ipswich and south Suffolk offers a range of leisure facilities, e.g. bike hire, boating, fishing, nature trails and a cafe. For information Tel. 01473–328408. Six pubs within easy reach of the reservoir.

WALK: With the lake to your right walk back towards Holbrook; take first footpath on left across a field into the churchyard, past two lovely old lime trees at the gate. At the road turn left down to

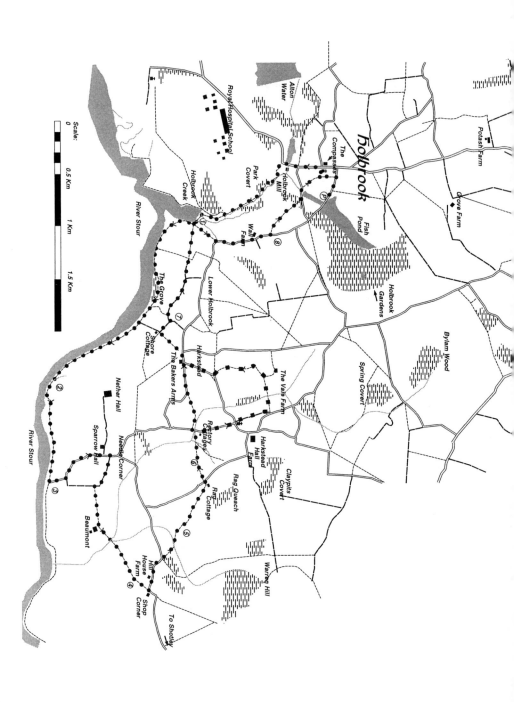

Holbrook Mill and along the boardwalk across the old mill pond. As the road turns sharply right take the path to the left. It meanders alongside the mill stream and reed beds, overhung with hazels and willows, to Holbrook Creek.

A splendid view across Holbrook Bay — the river is a mile wide here. The Royal Hospital School with its 200 foot spire is on a rise to the right. Established in Greenwich in 1712, for the education and maintenance of the sons of seamen, it moved to Holbrook in 1933.

1. Turn left along the track and right at the junction. Follow the path along the creek, lined with saltmarsh and sea lavender, then along the shore passing low sandy cliffs, some with exposed roots of thorn trees trailing down them. If the path is not clear, keep to the top of the beach.

Across the river is Copperas Bay. Copperas, from which iron sulphate was extracted to make ink and black dye — also the yellow colour used in house paint — was dredged up from the seabed in the bay and brought ashore here.

2. Where there is a very small inlet through the salt marsh, you will have to find a way across the marsh back on to the path. Follow the path along the cliff top, till you come to a hedge running inland and a footpath sign to your left. (This is about 2 miles from where you joined the shore path).

MILL STREAM PATH
HOLBROOK

3. Turn up here and, at a junction, turn left along a stony track towards some houses at Needle Corner. Turn right on to a footpath across the field with a deep drainage ditch to your left. At the paved lane go left of the farm buildings, (Beaumont Hall) diagonally downhill, through a kind of archway in the hedge. Cross a stile and footbridge then aim uphill towards the buildings.

It is rather hedgeless around here and several fields contain 2 or 3 different crops with no boundaries between them. A bit like the old strip fields perhaps.

4. Follow round the field to the top corner by a wire fence. Climb the stile on your left and cross some rough ground; over some low chicken wire and to a stile at the end of the field to the right. Cross it and turn left up to the road at Shop Corner. Turn left down the road and when it swings to the left continue ahead into the meadow and follow the broad track straight ahead. Just before the gate, bear left into an L shaped bit of field and through a gate at the bottom,(can be very muddy — stream running through) into another meadow with some old pollarded oaks by a stream bed.

5. Continue past a plantation of pine and sweet chestnut on your left and a pond full of bulrushes. Bear left to a stile; cross it and turn right to another footpath sign on your left attached to a non-existent path. Walk round the field edge to a track behind a hedge. Turn left along it skirting Rag Cottage. Cross a lane and take the path through the crop opposite. Aim for a slight gap in the hedge under the telegraph wires.

6. Cross the farm track and a fence at the gap in the hedge. Continue ahead over rough ground aiming towards Rectory Cottages slightly to your right. You pass a pond surrounded with brambles and briars and go through the gate to the road. Turn left and almost immediately right on to the footpath then cross the footbridge and follow the path through the field slightly left. At the road turn right into the village. Take a left turn immediately past the pub, Walnut Tree Lane. Follow the footpath sign to the right. The path goes downhill towards the river — lovely views. At Shore cottage turn right along the lane for about 100 yards.

7. Turn left across the field then branch right along the path to Holbrook Creek. Here turn right up the bridleway to the road and

turn left up the hill to just past the entrance to Wall Farm.

8. Take a footpath to the left; in front of the cottages veer off left ·over the field, across a track on to a pretty, windy downhill path through mixed woodland. At the road turn left and past the end of the lake turn right up towards the church. Cross the stile to your right and go diagonally across the field to another stile. Turn right into the lane and back to the layby.

LITTLE RINGED PLOVER

ALTERNATIVE WALK: At Rectory Cottages turn right up to the church; take the footpath to its left, through a gate, across a stile on to a path between fenced paddocks. Across another stile and a crop field where a signpost directs you to the left — then abandons you! Follow the track downhill towards the poplars. Cross the meadow and up the other side of the valley to Vale Farm. Bear left till you reach a road which leads into Harkstead. This will add about one mile to the walk.

The church is built mostly of local septaria. It has an avenue of splendid yews up to its door. Behind the altar is an unusual tile decoration of grapes and wheat — looks Portuguese.

SHORTER WALK: At Needle Corner turn left along the road to Rectory Cottages where you turn left, cross the footbridge and out to the road into Harkstead. (About 1 mile less). Really short walk: 4 miles. Start as directed and between 1. and 2. turn inland to Harkstead and return from pub as directed.

THE SANDLINGS

SHEEP ON SANDLINGS HEATH

Arthur Young, the 18th century agricultural writer, wrote of 'the Sandling' as the area "south of the line of Woodbridge and Orford..." where the soil was poor, blown, sand. But various demarcations of the area apply and for our purposes it is the area stretching roughly from Lowestoft to Ipswich and from the coast to the A12. It is made up of sands known as crags. The shelly Coralline Crag deposited in warm tropical conditions about 3.5 million years ago is the oldest; it forms a narrow island, in a sea of Red Crag, stretching from around Butley to north of Aldeburgh. The Red Crag which covers most of the Sandlings contains an abundance of fossil shells giving clues to the type of climate at the time it was laid down. The younger Norwich Crag occurs north of Orford and is less than 2 million years old. The Kesgrave sands and gravels which underlie much of the East Suffolk heathland are thought to have been deposited by a great river ancestral to the Thames which flowed north-eastward across Suffolk nearly a million years ago. Later deposits were left by retreating ice sheets which also helped to form the river valleys.

The character of the Sandlings is profoundly influenced by its four large river estuaries. They formed as a result of a combination of geological events around 7000 years ago. The North Sea basin subsided at the same time as the sea level rose — a result of the climate warming up after the last ice age. The rising sea swamped the river valleys creating the wide shallow estuaries we know today. It is these estuaries that have saved Suffolk from the sort of coastal development common elsewhere, where roads have been built for long distances following the coast line.

LAND SETTLEMENT AND USE

At one time there was abundant heathland along the eastern Sandlings; a result of abandoned cultivated land that could no longer support crops. Neolithic settlers had farmed the alluvial soils of the river valleys and as the population grew and they needed more land they felled the forest to create pastures and fields. As this became exhausted they abandoned it,moved on and felled more woodland. The abandoned farmland turned firstly to heath then, if not grazed or ploughed up again for agriculture, it grew birch and pine scrub and would finally become woodland. At the beginning of this century there were 160 square miles of heath between Lowestoft and Ipswich, now there are only 30 square miles, most of it concentrated in the areas north of Aldeburgh and east of Woodbridge.

Marshes fringing the rivers and coast were being drained to provide more farmland. Earth banks planted with coarse grasses to stabilize them were built with tidal sluices to control the water levels and for centuries cattle could be seen roaming the miles of grazing marshes. The Romans probably built the first sea wall but certainly the Normans built them later and a good deal of sea wall construction took place in the 16th and 17th centuries.

During the 18th and 19th centuries heathland came to be looked upon as a wasted resource and was enclosed to make farms larger, more efficient and easier to work. In the 20th century farming has continued to have the largest influence on the landscape, particularly in the estuaries. High concrete flood walls, built after the disastrous floods of January 1953, create their own problems as they do not dissipate the wave energy in the way saltmarsh does; saltmarsh won't easily establish itself in front of them as it does along the old grass banks. The marshes were extensively drained so arable land and dry pasture replaced both marsh and heath. The shallow valley sides have been stripped of trees and ploughed up to the valley floor.

In the 1920s the Forestry Commission planted Rendlesham Forest on acres of heathland and poor, sandy, arable land. This was devastated by the gales in 1987 just as it was reaching maturity. The 20th century has also seen great industrial and commercial development, from concrete runways for the wartime airfields at Woodbridge and Bentwaters to the tremendous spread of Felixstowe docks along the shingle beaches and saltmarshes of the Orwell estuary. Further areas of saltmarsh and mud flat have been overtaken by yacht marinas. Housing and industrial workshops have obliterated Martlesham Heath.

In 1988 The Sandlings was designated an Area of Outstanding Natural Beauty (AONB) which gave small livestock farmers an opportunity to expand and cattle and sheep can again be seen grazing on parts of the coast. It also encouraged tree planting and the reinstatement of landscape features. The Sandlings Group was set up in 1983 and it works closely with the Suffolk Coast and Heaths Project which came into being in 1993 to establish policies to restore the landscape, develop recreational opportunities and promote public awareness of the value of this vulnerable area.

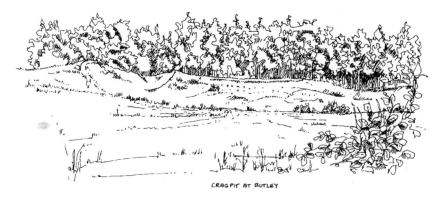

CRAGPIT AT BUTLEY

SPECIAL FEATURES

Most of the special features of the Sandlings result from its being a coastal area with miles of shingle beaches, a few sand dunes in the north, mudflats and saltmarsh along the estuaries. Of the four largest rivers of the Sandlings the Orwell has the deepest, widest and straightest estuary with comparatively steep, fairly well-wooded slopes. It provides a deep dredged channel from the sea to Ipswich, an important port since the 9th century. Moving northwards the river valleys become shallower with wide drained marshy flats between very gently rising slopes. The Deben is tranquil and unspoilt for most of its length, mainly because there are very few places you can reach it by car. Its south side is bordered by reed beds, saltmarsh and mudflats with fields behind the ancient flood walls. Along the northern shore are a number of sandy beaches and crumbling orange cliffs. Below Ramsholt the land opens out into flat arable plains with remnants of saltings. As it reaches the sea the river narrows and is constrained between shingle banks.

The Alde rises near Laxfield in High Suffolk and widens into a broad tidal estuary of mud flats and reed beds just east of Snape Bridge. At Iken Cliff the south shore rises and beyond this are the low hills that were once islands. Yarn Hill, thatched with pines, was once a Stone Age settlement. As the river reaches Aldeburgh it narrows and turns sharply south running parallel to the coast between the shingle spit of Orford Ness and Sudbourne marshes. South of Orford it becomes the Ore and is joined by the Butley river before reaching the sea at Shingle Street.

The Blyth has a very narrow mouth contained by the flood defences protecting Southwold harbour and the village of Walberswick. Like the Alde it bends sharply inland and opens out into a vast expanse of mud flats where it has broken through the flood defences. It contracts suddenly at Blythburgh amongst the reed beds at the foot of the most imposing church. Several smaller rivers such as the Minsmere and two called the Hundred have silted up and been cut off from the sea by shingle bars. Sea water seeps through the shingle and sometimes over-tops it forming brackish lagoons where rivers once ran; as at Benacre, Covehithe and Easton, between Lowestoft and Southwold.

The RSPB reserve fills the shallow marshy pools of the old Minsmere river and at Aldeburgh one of the rivers Hundred trickles into the sea through a sluice at the edge of North Warren nature reserve. It once formed the medieval haven of Aldeburgh. At that time Dunwich was the biggest port on the Suffolk cost, equal in size to Norwich, until in the 13th century great storms threw up shingle which blocked the river, diverting its course. It now wanders along the coast behind a shingle bar, through Westwood marshes to debouch into the Blyth river at Walberswick.

The Coast. The coast is very open and exposed to tides, currents and winds — it is a very dynamic area with constantly shifting shingle banks and soft eroding cliffs which form patches of sandy beach with fallen trees and other debris at the base of the cliffs affording a home for grass and other plants.

Dunwich has disappeared into the sea at the rate of about 400 metres in the last 400 years. In the same period Orford Ness has grown about three miles. Shingle is shifted south along the coast by waves generated by the north-easterly winds. Some of the original pebbles were probably supplied by cliff erosion at Dunwich. Down the coast at Bawdsey the remains of a forest lie out to sea and across the mouth of the Deben an old Roman fort lies off shore. It is thought that the cliffs of Felixstowe, in Roman times, were about a mile further out to sea. Natural erosion by the elements has been aided by the excavation of septaria for building stone over the centuries.

NATURAL HISTORY

Orford Ness. Some 15km long, is the best vegetated shingle spit in Europe and both it and Landguard are SSSIs because of their rare and important plant communities. Shingle provides a surprising variety of habitats. Where it is more stable, above the high water mark, a few plants take root where they can get a hold in finer grains between the pebbles. As the plants shed bits or die they decompose and humus accumulates, allowing more plants to establish. Gradually quite a variety of species develops until, in places, you get

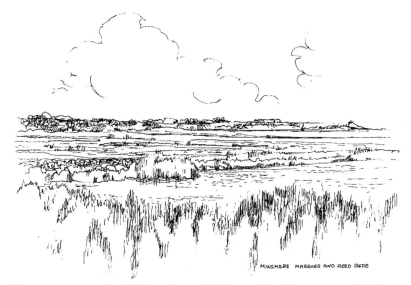

MINSMERE MARSHES AND REED BEDS

a thin covering of acid heath turf. The early pioneer species have to contend with pretty severe conditions and therefore have adopted clever coping mechanisms. Many specialist species are very localised and often quite rare; for example sea pea, sea kale, yellow horned poppy, stinking goosefoot, clustered and suffocated clovers. Flowering plants attract butterflies including the holly blue, clouded yellow and painted lady. Plant growth is encouraged by the birds that breed on shingle sites, providing nutrients to the shingle plants.

Intertidal mudflats: These vast expanses of tidally exposed mud in the river estuaries provide a harsh environment for wildlife. In the summer they can support algae and eel grass but in winter waves and tides scour the surface and cause erosion. Temperature, salinity and turbidity are in a continual state of flux. The only animals who live in this environment are invertebrates who can burrow into the mud or close their shells when conditions become intolerable. Many species can adapt their body fluids in response to changing salinity. Mudflats contain, as well as mud and silt deposits, plants from sea and river which provide food for the many molluscs, crustaceans and polychaete worms which in turn provide abundant food for fish and numerous flocks of waders and wildfowl. The flats are threatened, collectively, by dock and marina activities, waste disposal and wildfowling. The Orwell and Stour have suffered the worst erosion, probably due to a mix of factors including shipping using the ports of Felixstowe, Harwich and Ipswich.

Saltmarsh: Salt tolerant grassland on muddy sediments provides an important transitional vegetated area between tidal mudflats and dry land. Saltmarsh plants have developed some ingenious tricks and devices to enable them to tolerate saline conditions and they act as sediment traps, catching silt and sand from river water. As it builds up, saltmarsh often forms a low cliff allowing a mixed community of plants to become established. There are 3 levels of marsh. Low marsh lying below the average low tide mark, where only green algae and sometimes eel grass survive. As the marsh grades into middle marsh you get glasswort, cord grass and sea aster; then sea purslane, sea lavender, sea arrow grass, sea milkwort, sea rush and saltmarsh grass. The middle marsh is mostly submerged every tidal cycle and the soil is waterlogged with salt water. In the high marsh the soil may dry out completely as it is only submerged briefly when tides are higher than average. Here you find sea couch and members of the Goosefoot family such as sea beet. It is characteristic of saltmarsh that the surface is split by a network of tidal drainage creeks and salt pans. Left to develop naturally saltmarsh would progress to grazing marsh and to carr if not grazed. In Suffolk this is mostly prevented by the sea walls. Saltmarsh is very important for birds, providing grazing for over-wintering flocks of widgeon and brent-geese. It provides roosting sites for waders and nesting sites for such as redshank, avocet, oystercatcher, skylark and meadow pipit and seed heads for linnet and twite to feed on. The Deben has the largest remaining amount of saltmarsh, then the Alde/Ore/Butley complex.

Coastal grazing marsh: Saltmarsh that was 'inned' was no longer salt and so made very good grazing for cattle and sheep. It stretched all along the coast and river estuaries from at least the enclosures until 1953 when the floods broke through the sea walls and swamped them. Several years later the marsh land was 'improved' — levelled, underdrained and chemically farmed behind the rebuilt walls. Fragments of unimproved marsh remained to be managed in the traditional way, for example Tinkers Marsh at Walberswick and

Sizewell Belts. Some of the improved marshes are now reverting to traditional management. Hazelwood marshes at Aldeburgh and Trimley Marshes are examples.

Reedbeds have developed in the upper reaches of estuaries, notably on the Butley, Alde and Blythe rivers and where grazing has stopped on coastal marshes, such as Westwood. Reedbeds are one of the first steps in a succession from water to woodland. They grow with a proportion of their stalks below water. When they die they eventually rot and form a peaty soil. The litter from dead reeds raises the reed bed higher above the water level, then fen and scrub develop. Reeds tolerate a variety of soils but they are not keen on salt water. Reed beds can be maintained by rotational cropping in winter and removal of scrub. Summer cutting of green reeds reduces growth and prevents encroachment.

Heaths: The heathers of the sandlings are mainly ling (*Calluna vulgaris*) and bell heather (*Erica cinerea*), the latter thriving in hot, dry conditions. If the heather is heavily grazed various grasses will take over creating grassy heathland. If heather is being reinstated it needs to be seeded and Dunwich heath is usually the source of seed. The older heather is cut in October and November when the seed is ripe, then baled and taken to the new site and spread out in a layer so the seeds fall to the ground and germinate. As mature heather is scarce — it takes 20 years to reach the stage when you can afford to cut it — experiments are being done in which the seed is 'hoovered' off younger heather and spread where it is needed to grow. The heather on Dunwich Heath was in a very poor state this summer(1996), one theory being that the weather has been too dry to wash off the salt spray from winter storms.

At various times farmers have ploughed up the heathland to plant crops, usually trying to improve the soil by adding marl in the shape of crag, gravel or lime. But in a very short time the land proved too poor and was allowed to revert to heath. However by adding tons of artificial fertilizers, 20th century farmers have been successful in producing high yields of cereals and other crops. But much of the land is almost pure sand which in the spring winds is blown about in great dust storms, drifting deeply at the roadsides.

Woodland: There are a great many small woods, tiny coverts and shelter belts. There are the vast tracts of Forestry Commission conifers, Scots and Corsican pine and Douglas fir. In spite of the devastation caused by the 1987 gales the forests have benefited as it has allowed a more enlightened approach. Fallen trees have been cleared into 'windrows' and left to rot, providing habitats for a great variety of wildlife including insects, bacteria and other micro-organisms which all help to decompose the dead trees, providing both soil nutrients and organic matter to improve the soil structure. New trees have been planted between the windrows including some broad leafed hardwoods. Clearings have been left in places, allowing in more light to encourage flowering plants to get established. In turn these attract butterflies and moths.

These woods are extensively managed by Forest Enterprise who encourage people to both use and learn from them. They provide leaflets of walks and nature trails as well as picnic places.

There are still one or two patches of ancient woodland, notably Staverton Thicks, just by Rendlesham Forest, with its 400 year old pollarded oaks and hollies, almost untouched by the gales.

WINDROW IN RENDLESHAM FOREST

134

16. NACTON TO LEVINGTON

Along the northern shore of the Orwell from the cliffs at Nacton to the saltmarshes around Levington. Through woods and arable land — some steep slopes — and river wall.

Distance: 7.2 km (4.5 miles) or 13.5 km (8.5 miles).

Map: Pathfinder 1054.

Start: Park off the road by the footpath sign opposite the northern end of Levington Research station. GR 240401.

Buses: Limited service on Ipswich to Felixstowe route. Eastern Counties.

WHERE TO EAT
Levington, Ship Inn. Old smugglers inn. Egon Ronay Healthy Eating award. Very popular so can be crowded. Garden at back, tables out front. Tel. 01473–659573.

LOCAL INTEREST
Nacton Meadows Nature Reserve, (SWT) SSSI. Sandy meadow with broom, oaks, brambles leads steeply down to valley bottom full of meadowsweet, rushes, marsh marigold, lesser spearwort and masses of southern marsh and common spotted orchids in season. Frogs and toads around the stream — sometimes grass snakes can be seen. Cattle graze in summer.
Levington Lagoon, small wetland reserve next to flood wall on longer walk.
Trimley Marshes, GR 258355. Reserve created as a condition of the Felixstowe dock extension. Grazing wet meadows and two fresh-water lagoons with islands, reedbeds. Breeding, passage and wintering wading birds and wildfowl.

WALK: Walk towards Levington village. Shortly after the village sign there are two footpaths on the right — by a sign 'Danger Children' — one goes to the nature reserve, well worth a visit.
    1. Take the left hand path downhill into a pretty valley and along

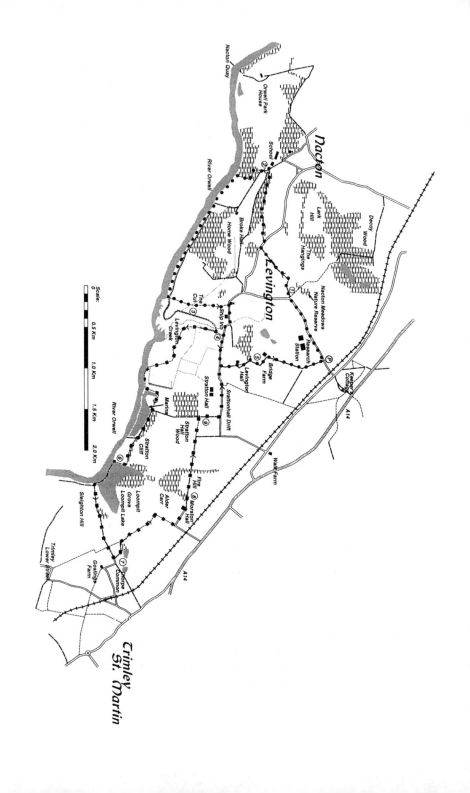

a field side. At the road turn right for a few yards then left on to a path that wanders through carr woodland, crossing the stream 2 or 3 times. It curves to the left, leaving the wood in front of the entrance to Broke Hall.

2. Follow the track to Nacton Picnic Site. At the river turn left — there is a path along the grass and over the cliffs but this is on private land and is not a public Right of Way. You should walk along the sandy, pebbly foreshore. Take note of the tides, some parts may not be passable at high tide.

The vegetated cliffs reach 20 metres in height and are dramatically eroded in places with fallen trees lying on the beach. Very attractive route.

Just after the saltings start, near Levington Creek, take a footpath heading inland across the field towards the pretty church at Levington.

3. A footbridge crosses The Cut and a board walk continues ahead through the marshes. Opposite the pub turn right and follow the lane down past the head of the creek on the right.

4. Levington Creek was once a hive of activity. In the 13th century shrimp and mussel beds in the creek provided large quantities of fish for the Ipswich market. In the 14th century an Admiralty Court which adjudicated on all matters maritime was held here and later on Thames barges delivered bricks and exported coprolite and grain. At the beginning of the 18th century coprolite was first used in Levington, for a fertilizer, 100 years or more before the industry became a commercial success. The research station was built by Fisons in the 1950s — they began their agricultural business with the coprolite trade in the 19th century.

Continue up hill and down again where you will find a track to the left. At the back of Levington Hall branch right into trees.

5. Follow alongside the paddock to Bridge Farm, then turn right and continue along the broad track, past the research station and cross the road to your car.

FOR A LONGER WALK. Go down the road from the pub but turn right towards the head of the creek (**4**). Follow the river wall to the marina. Continue through the marina and opposite the

Yacht Club take the path up the cliff and through the trees. This brings you down to a causeway between Loompit lake and the river.

6. Cross the causeway to a sandy beach at the far end and turn left on to the track up Sleighton Hill; continue till you are near the end of Thorpe Lane, about half a mile.

7. Take a bridleway to the left then cross a stile to the right and follow the footpath downhill through the trees. At the bottom turn right uphill to some cottages on a sandy track. Continue on this track to just before the level crossing and turn left on to Morston Hall track.

8. Follow the waymarks through the farm and continue straight ahead, through a hedge, down a slope then up another one at the edge of a vast field.

9. At the road turn right then left into Strattonhall Drift. Continue along here until you reach the footpath on the right towards Levington Hall. Continue as from (**5**).

NACTON SHORE

138

17. SUTTON AND RIVER DEBEN

VIEW UP THE DEBEN
FROM SUTTON SHORE

Delightful varied walk by the river, through woods, marshes, farm-land, heathland and along the cliff top. Some tricky bits.

Distance: 13.5 km (8.5 miles).

Map: Pathfinder 1031.

Start: Car park at the corner of B1083 and the Hollesley road GR 298491.

Buses: Regular services from Woodbridge. Eastern Counties Tel. 01473–253734.

WHERE TO EAT
Sutton, The Plough. Usual bar meals including vegetarian. Big gar-

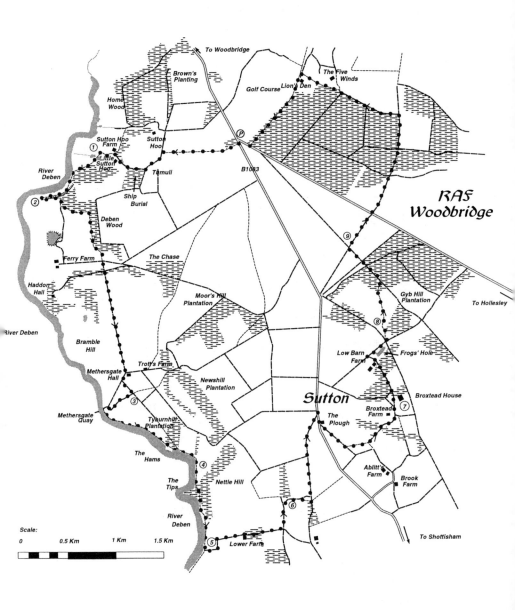

den and vine covered terrace. Tel. 01394–411785.

LOCAL INTEREST
Sutton Hoo Burial Site, (National Trust). 7th century royal Anglo-Saxon burial site. Wooden warship and others treasures. Display of maps, models etc. on site. **Woodbridge Museum** contains exhibits of Sutton Hoo, and Burrow Hill excavations. Most of the Sutton Hoo treasure is in the British Museum. For details consult Woodbridge Tourist Information, Station Buildings. Tel. 01394–382240.

WALK: Go down the path leading to the ship burial site. As you pass this turn right on the marked path down towards the river, passing the left side of Sutton Hoo Farm.

1. The track leads between 2 ponds, past a pump house, alongside a meadow with a wood to the left. Cross a footbridge on to the river wall. The path to the left meanders near the foot of the cliff between the trees and it can be very slippery when wet.

2. You come to some steps leading up the cliff; at the top turn left along the field side. Beautiful views here across the river to Woodbridge and Melton. Follow the bridleway round the edge of the wood and at the end, by 3 pines, head off slightly to the right across the field. Cross the drives to Ferry Farm and Haddon Hall.

If you want just a short walk turn left at Ferry Farm drive; left at the next fork back to the road. Turn left back to car park.

Continue ahead till you reach the back of the house at Methersgate. Turn right and immediately left between 2 buildings and down a path, then left at a brick wall.

3. At a signpost directing you left or right cross the stile to the right, down to Methersgate Quay where you turn right, left and left again along the river bank till you come to a stile by a wood. Cross into the wood and follow the path to a hill. It's easiest to descend to the beach and walk round The Hams, along the beach to the concrete river wall.

4. Follow the path along the wall, through the wood on Nettle Hill. When it peters out, take to the beach again.

The Hams and The Tips were built out into the river during the late 19th century by Robert Knipe Cobbold in an attempt to reclaim 150 acres of Saltings for farmland. He'd intended they

should reach further out into the river but Trinity House put a stop to these plans, afraid they'd alter the course of the river and interfere with shipping.

5. When the reed beds start follow the very narrow path running along the back of them and up the cliff, into a field which you cross to join the farm track; turn left. After 2 gates you reach a cross tracks; turn left and when you come to a spinney turn right.

6. Pass, on your right, an old pit with bulrushes growing in it. At the paved lane turn left and just before the main road cut through between the houses to the right, coming out opposite the pub. Immediately to the right of the pub a footpath leads you between back gardens and a field. Turn left out of the field into the lane and follow it round to the right.

The land around here is in the Countryside Stewardship scheme and notice boards invite you into the fields.

7. At a triangle go left past some houses and carry straight on past the gates of Broxtead House — following the sandy track as it bears slightly left, past a rather dry pond (Frogs Hole) to a sparse hedge where you turn right towards some Scots pines. Follow the signposted path towards a small pine plantation; at its corner bear left along the main track.

8. Very soon branch off to the right over the heath along a slight depression in the ground, rather than a track. Enter the wood and turn left on to a broad track which you follow through the wood, across the heath to a fenced crop field.

9. Turn right and on reaching the main road cross straight over and continue ahead on the track with the wire fence of Woodbridge airfield to the right.

Notice the soil profile of the ditch on the left. Very sandy with stones with a few inches of organic top soil formed from rotted vegetation.

Keep to the track as it follows the edge of the wood, turning left along the wood till you come to the golf course. Turn left down to the road.

The track here goes through an area that has been forested in the past — tree stumps and decomposed wind rows remain. Turn right back to the car park.

18. BUTLEY — ORFORD — SUDBOURNE

An easy walk on wide sandy tracks through some of the quietest Suffolk countryside; by marshes, through woods and arable land and across remote Butley Creek. Idyllic in summer it can be bleak and wild in winter.

Distance: 14.5 km (9 miles).

Map: Pathfinder 1008, 1031 and 1009.

Start: Park at Butley church GR 374503 — room for 1 or 2 cars. From Orford; park outside school GR 419502.

Buses: Limited service from Ipswich, Woodbridge and Saxmundham. Tel. Eastern Counties 01473–253734.

WHERE TO EAT
Orford, The Kings Head. Old beamed pub. Large interesting menu with vegetarian choices. Garden. Tel. 01394– 450271.
Jolly Sailor. Unspoilt traditional local. Large garden with views over Gedgrave Marshes. Good value. Excellent fish and chips. Tel. 01394–450243.
Crown and Castle Hotel. Comfortable old hotel. Bar snacks, morning coffee, afternoon tea. Tel. 01394–450205.
Butley Orford Oysterage. Great variety of fish dishes and locally grown oysters. Tel. 01394–450277
Old Warehouse Tea Shop. Excellent home-made cakes and scones. Lunches, licensed. Summer, open every day except Monday. Winter, Thursday and Friday 10.00–3.30. Week-ends 10–5. Tel. 01394–450210 .
Chillesford, Froize Inn. Former 'local' now known for its food. Closed Monday lunchtime. Tel. 01394–450282.
Butley, Oyster Inn. Simply furnished pleasant pub. Small garden. Traditional food. Tel. 01394–450790.
Butley Barns, Mill Lane. Tea room, pottery shop and gallery with regularly changing exhibitions. Open daily 10.30–5.00 Easter to end September. 11.00–4.00 Wednesday–Sunday, October to

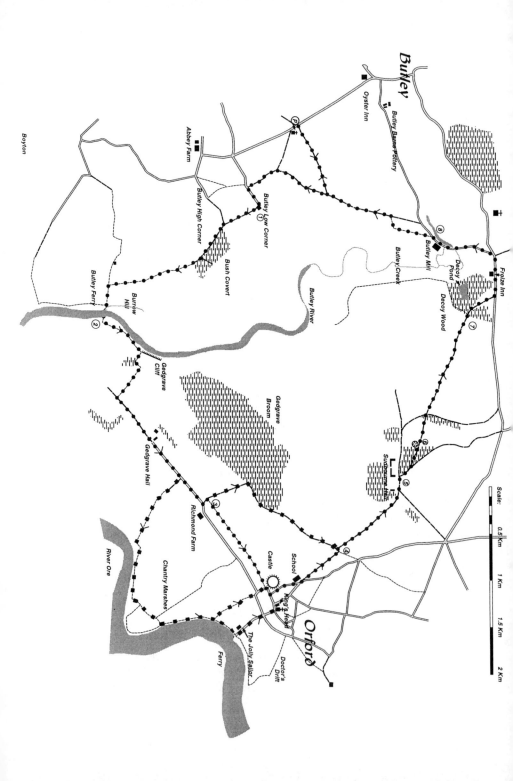

December, January closed. Tel. 01394–450785.

LOCAL INTEREST
Butley Ferry. On the site of the medieval ferry built by the priors
of Butley and recently rebuilt by Mr. Rogers. He will be only too
pleased to row you across. Please ring the day before you want to
go, if possible. Cost £1 per adult; children and dogs 50p each. Tel.
01394–410096.
Orford Castle. Open daily 10.00–6.00 April to end September.
October–end March 10 to 1pm and 2 to 4pm. Tel. 01394– 450472.
Orford Museum. Old stable behind the Crown and Castle. Open
April–September daily 2–4pm. Tel. 01394–450421.
Boat Trips. Round Havergate Island. Daily, weather permitting.
Tel. 01394–450637. Alde/Ore river trips. Food and bar on board.
Book at Old Warehouse or Tel. 01831–698298.
Havergate Island Nature Reserve, (RSPB). Limited access by boat
from Orford Quay, March–September. Tickets from John Partridge,
30 Mundays Lane, Orford, IP12 2LX.
Orford Ness National Nature Reserve, (English Nature). Access
on foot only. No dogs, fires or camping because of fragile nature of
habitat.
Orford Ness Reserve, (National Trust). Ferry from Orford Quay.
Small charge for visitors. Tel. 01394–450057.

WALK: Take the footpath signposted along the north side of
Butley church to a T junction; turn right along the by way to the
lane at Butley Low corner. Turn left by a converted chapel and pass
a pond on the left, overgrown with brambles and willows.

1. At the end of the lane turn right and continue ahead across the
fields towards Bush covert.

**There was a field on the left marked 'High value cash crop —
keep out'. It was the most beautiful outsize lawn! Turf is grown
as a crop in several places in the area.**

Continue on past Bush covert, over arable land to the marshes
which you cross to reach Burrow Hill.

**Around here in medieval times were the fields tended by the
priors of Butley Abbey which stood over to your right where
Abbey Farm now is. Orford Ness was way north of Orford and
the river mouth stretched from around Boyton to Gedgrave cliff.**

ORFORD ACROSS THE RECLAIMED MARSHES

Here the land is only 2–3 metres above sea level. It is covered with a network of drainage ditches but before Orford Ness cut Butley river off from the sea the low lying land must often have been under water. Burrow Hill was a Saxon island settlement. Excavations in 1983 unearthed coffins containing bodies, a small kiln and other artefacts, dated from AD780 to AD830.

Climb Burrow Hill and descend slightly to the right, over a stile and turn left towards the river wall at the ferry.

2. Cross on the ferry, having rung Mr Rogers to arrange it. Disembark on the Gedgrave side and turn left along the creek side for a scant quarter of a mile, past the oyster beds. Turn inland towards a small wood where you turn left then right. Continue down to Gedgrave Lane and turn left, then left again just before Richmond Farm.

3. Where the land rises climb the steps up the bank to the right. Good views over the marshes and Orford Ness with its old military installations. Walk towards Orford castle; cross three crop fields all with clear paths through them. Follow round a bungalow

146

to a gravel drive; cross this and continue ahead passing an old crag pit on the left, and over the castle earthworks, through the car park and into the village square where you turn left, passing the excellent village stores and continuing up to the school. Go past the school and straight ahead till you reach a cross tracks.

4. Continue straight ahead between a cottage and a gate. Follow the path between vegetable fields and the cricket pitch.

5. Pass Sudbourne Hall on the left and take the footpath to the right beneath an avenue of chestnuts. After a short distance turn left on to a path into some conifers.

6. Leaving the trees the path runs along the rim of an old crag pit and continues through the crop — there are shells in the sand.

The land all around here, is almost pure sand. At Butley it is very orange, here it is more buff-grey. It is very productive, mostly vegetables, but must require a great deal of fertilizer as some fields yield three crops a year. For example carrots followed by beans then wheat.

The path continues through a patch of scrub, then on to another broad sandy track more or less straight ahead, through what was the park of Sudbourne Hall and there are several horse chestnut avenues. Cross a tarmac drive and continue ahead through a small sweet chestnut plantation, then between two fields.

7. You come to a signpost to the left which leads past the decoy pond and down through the marshland along Butley Creek. An interesting path but a dead end, so continue straight ahead to the road at Chillesford and turn left, past the Froize Inn and left into Mill Lane. There are glimpses of the mill pond through the trees to the right.

8. Just past the Mill buildings turn left over some concrete, up a grassy track and cross the field ahead.

Great views of Butley Creek to the left; for centuries busy with barges carrying corn to the mill for grinding. Barge traffic ceased in 1914 when the river finally silted up and became choked with reeds.

At the hedge at the bottom of the field turn right to the broad sandy track, on which you turn left.

The fields on either side of this track are enormous, hedgeless

147

seas of sand. Some wind-blown ridges of sand have formed with grass beginning to grow on them forming dunes.

When the track divides follow the right hand one back to the church. You pass the site of the original settlement next to the church. It is thought to have vanished with the Black Death. On the other side of the church is the school, closed only a few years ago.

ALTERNATIVE ROUTES. From Gedgrave Lane, just before Richmond Farm, turn right across the marshes to the banks of the Ore opposite Havergate island. This route might appeal to birders. Follow the river bank to Orford Quay where you can either walk into the village, up to the school and continue to Sudbourne, or take the footpath behind the Old Warehouse Tea Shop and continue along the river wall to a footbridge where you turn left across the marshes and along Doctors Drift, an old sheep or cattle drove, that brings you out on Daphne Road. Wander through the village to the school and so on to Sudbourne.

If you do not want to go into Orford; at (3) continue straight ahead past some Scots pines towards the gloomy conifer plantation (Gedgrave Broom) where you turn right and follow the yellow waymarks to the junction (4) where you turn left between the house and gate.

19. DUNWICH TO WALBERSWICK

Interesting, varied walk but well trodden. Through Dunwich forest, Walberswick National Nature Reserve, the vast reed beds of Westwood Marshes — can be very muddy, boots essential — and along the Dunwich river.

Distance: 12km (7.5 miles).

Map: Pathfinder 966.

Start: Car park, Dunwich Beach GR 478706.

Buses: Dunwich, limited service, Tel. Wayland Minibus Services 01502–716989. Walberswick, Eastern Counties from Lowestoft, Wednesdays and Fridays. Tel. 01502–565406.

WHERE TO EAT
Dunwich, The Ship. Wide selection of home-made meals; vegetarian and local fish dishes. Large garden. Tel. 01728– 648219.
Flora Tea Rooms. Large airy beach cafe, renowned for its fish and chips. Open during season 10–5; other times 10–3; closed November to early March.
Walberswick, The Bell, near village green. Old pub with stone flags, high backed settles. Excellent home cooked food; vegetarian choices. Tel. 01502–723109.
The Anchor, residential hotel; good bar meals. Small garden. Tel. 01502–722112.
Mary's of Walberswick, High Street. Cream teas, high teas and lunches. Open Easter–October, Tuesday–Sunday 10–6. Mondays during summer holidays. November–Easter, open Friday–Sunday. Tel. 01502–723243.
Parish Lantern, on The Green. Craft shop with Tearoom. Open, Summer 10–5 every day. January–March, Friday– Sunday. Tel. 01502–723173.

LOCAL INTEREST
Dunwich Museum, St.James Street. Good little museum, with model of the medieval town and its relation to today's coastline. Open daily Good Friday to September, 11.30–4.40; October 12–4;

March, weekends only 2.00.–4.30.

Greyfriars Franciscan Friary, on the cliff top. The track along the cliff marks the western boundary of the old town when the friary was built in 1289.

Walberswick to Southwold ferry, Summer, 9.00.–12.30 and 2.00.–5.30. Nearby: Blythburgh Church, aptly called the cathedral of the marshes, it is as impressive inside as out. **Minsmere Reserve,** RSPB. Just south of Dunwich Heath, Open daily, except Tuesday. Visitor Centre, cafe, shop. Tel. 01728–648281. **Dunwich Heath,** National Trust reserve; Teashop, information room, lookout and shop. In old coastguards' cottages.

WALK: From car park walk along the main street and just past the church take the footpath to the left along the lane, a good track between burgeoning hedges.

1. Shortly after passing Sandy Lane Farm turn right into a broad ride on the right with a forest walk sign. At a cross junction turn right between conifers which become infested with rhododendrons either side of the track. Cross the Dunwich river and follow the track round to the right, up to an open space with a confluence of tracks.

2. Keep straight ahead to the car park and picnic place. Cross it to the road and bear left.

3. Very shortly turn right on to a forest ride (a notice welcomes walkers). The straight track runs through a young pine plantation. At the first junction turn left on to the bridleway; at the next junction turn right and left at the one after to a broad stony track. Turn right to the end of the track with Dingle marshes in front.

Dunwich over to the right appears to stand quite high. Between here and the sea the Dunwich river runs parallel to the coast and into the mouth of the Blyth which in medieval times ran into Dunwich Haven. The Dunwich river was deflected northwards in the late 13th century when violent storms blocked the harbour with sand and shingle. Some years later the Blyth broke through the spit at Walberswick.

4. Turn left, pass a white clapboard house (Sole Bay Lodge). The very broad path goes between trees, hedges with marsh and sea to the right and to the left, Westwood Marshes, one of the largest stretches of freshwater reed beds in the country.

5. At a carved plaque showing 3 routes go more or less ahead past a cottage on the left with reed beds to the right. Follow the path along the edge of the reed beds up on to the causeway.

6. Follow the footpath across the causeway and to the left of a small hill.

The reedbeds stretch for miles, edged with scrub and bracken covered low sandy hills. Beautiful in the sunshine.

When you reach the river follow it to the wind pump, across a style. Turn right across the footbridge and continue along the river.

7. When you come to some high ground on the left — go onto it.

8. At a bridge over the river the path turns inland. Take a narrow path to the left through reeds towards a small hill and turn right on to a hard gravel track — continue ahead, past another bridge over the river and on into the village just by the public toilets. Turn right to the Bell, the river Blyth and the ferry to Southwold.

Early this century fishing was thriving with a herring and sprat curing business shared with Southwold. As this declined the artists moved in and it is still a popular place with artists.

To return, from the Blyth, follow the road past the village green to the side of the Anchor Hotel where you turn left on to the footpath.

9. At a field turn left towards the sea and follow

SPRAT SMOKING SHED
WALBERSWICK

the field edge to a derelict shed; turn left. At the next junction turn right, keeping the field to the right and reedbeds to the left.

10. The path winds around on higher ground through gorse, broom, bracken, brambles and tree lupins — great views over the marshes out to sea. At a T junction go left on to a board walk through Old Town Marshes and aim towards the wind pump.

Around here was the early medieval fishing port of Walberswick where ships traded with Iceland and the Baltic. But the later depredations of Henry VIII, a rapacious 17th century landlord, who appropriated the commons and quays for himself, and two devastating fires, put paid to Walberswick's earlier prosperity.

Retrace your steps from here, right, over the marshes, past the cottage, and the lane to the right where you joined this track.

11. Continue straight ahead back to Dunwich. Very good broad track with woods to the right and views of Dunwich over the marshes to the left.

There is a shingle bank running from Dunwich to Walberswick which has to be regularly maintained. Nevertheless erosion is quite severe. Chunks of marshland break off. Salt water flooding the marshes kills fish, small mammals, amphibians and insects that live in the reeds. Reeds have to be cut regularly to prevent succession. Water depth is important and should be kept at around 10 centimetres to maintain healthy reed beds.

The track ends at Bridge Farm — a plant nursery. Turn left on to the road into and through Dunwich to the car park.

20. SOUTH COVE — COVEHITHE

COVEHITHE CLIFFS

A walk through lanes and countryside little changed since the 1930s; through the reed beds of Pottersbridge marshes and the meadows between Cove Bottom and Frostenden Bottom. It is well worth taking in Covehithe Broad and the beach of the Benacre Nature Reserve though this is on private land and to follow the walk described you must return to the church by the same route. Easy going, well signposted.

Distance: 11.5 km (7 miles).

Map: Pathfinder 966 and 946.

Start: Park near Covehithe church. GR 523817.

Buses: A regular service runs along the A12 stopping at Wrentham. Eastern Counties, Tel. 01473–253734 or 01502– 565406. Join the

route from the footpath at (6).

WHERE TO EAT
South Cove, Five Bells. Excellent traditional home-made food, cooked to order. Pleasant garden.

LOCAL INTEREST
Benacre National Nature Reserve. (English Nature). Coastal reserve includes the broads of Benacre, Covehithe and Easton. Sand and shingle beaches with ever-eroding cliffs. Dunes, heaths, woodland and marsh. Breeding birds include little tern, bittern and marsh harrier. The land is privately owned and you can reach it only by concessionary paths along the beach and 2 public footpaths.
In Roman times the shore along here was about 2 miles further east and formed a ness. The long shore drift of shingle and sand blocked the river Easton helping to form the broads. The cliffs are now eroding at a rate of about 3 metres a year.
St. Andrews Church, Covehithe. The large ruin is a result of the church having always been far too big; the village couldn't afford to maintain it when the herring fishery slumped, so the smaller church was built inside it in the 17th century using material from the original church.
In the 14th century the land here belonged to John de Cove who had a quay, or hithe, built for loading and unloading goods. It was quite a busy fishing port with boats sailing to Iceland.
Reydon Wood, (SWT) GR 480788. Ancient woodland with bluebells and orchids and many other flowers. Several small mammals.
Wrentham Basketware. London Road, Wrentham. English willow basketmaking workshop and shop. Tel. 01502– 675628.

WALK: To visit the reserve, take the path opposite Covehithe church and though you must return the same way it would be a pity not to visit this unique site.

1. On return, turn left for about 0.5km then left on to a green track between hedges of trees and bracken; continue almost to Warren House. Turn sharp right until another junction in front of a pine plantation.

Good views here across the marshes to sand dunes behind the beach and the sea.

2. Turn left and at the next wood turn right then sharp left at the

next junction. Cross a footbridge into the marshes (part of the nature reserve). Follow the path to the right as it wanders through the reedbeds. There are a few footbridges in the more boggy bits.

In 1938 a very high tide flooded the marshes, depositing herrings on the lawn of Reydon Grove Farm!

At the road turn into the lane nearly opposite; it meanders through arable land on the right and meadows to the left, bordering the marshes.

These meadows used to be full of wild flowers but have long since been 'improved'. Many clumps of nettles testify to the quality of the soil.

3. You pass South Cove brickworks on the left and, just past the red phone box, turn left along the field track.

4. When the track turns left, by a telephone pole, head over the field, slightly to the right towards the wood.

The field here is very short cropped grass with moss and lichen with short flowering plants — like grassy heath.

Climb the stile; pass through the poplars, over a footbridge into a marshy meadow; across another footbridge over a very pretty stream. Cross another stile into a wooded pasture; at a tree bearing a yellow arrow turn right and along a dry shady path to the next lane where you turn right.

5. At a junction of 4 roads with a sign post, carry on towards South Cove.

To the left is Frostenden Bottom with remains of claypits used for making bricks and pottery.

Cross a stream and pass the footpath sign to the left, continue to the next left turning, Golden Square Lane. Follow this peaceful green track all the way to the B1123 and turn left.

This lane once formed the boundary of a large green which stretched away to the left and ahead to Wrentham.

6. A short distance past the Five Bells take the footpath on the right; towards the end of the field bear right to enter the next field half way along the hedge. Continue ahead till you come to Green Lane. Turn right.

7. You are now crossing what was Covehithe heath.

Continue down to the road and turn left back to the church.

ALTERNATIVE WALKS. To include a visit to Benacre nature reserve without having to retrace your steps to continue the described walk you have these choices:

1. Take the footpath from the church down through the nature reserve. At the beach walk north past Benacre Broad to the footpath leading inland just before the water filled pits at The Denes. After a mile and a bit turn left and follow the lane via Wood Farm, turning left at Park Farm and left again at Mill Lane and right into Green Lane opposite Holly Grove. This is a distance of about 6.5 miles.

In 1786 a hoard of over 900 Roman coins in a stone bottle was found by a workman at Benacre Broad.

2. Turn south at the beach, to Easton Lane then right on to the Lowestoft road, across Potters Bridge. Turn right a short distance ahead across the marshes and follow the way marks over the fields back to Covehithe road, then right back to the church. A total of about 6 miles. At Potters Bridge you could continue on to the lane on the left and continue the described walk from there.

Both these alternatives, added to the described walk would make interesting day-long walks of around 13 miles.

SELECTED BIBLIOGRAPHY AND FURTHER READING

Armstrong, Patrick *The Changing Landscape*, Terence Dalton 1975
Bacon, J & S. *The Suffolk Shoreline and the Sea*, Segment 1984
Beardall,C.H. and Casey,D.J. *Suffolk's Changing Countryside*, Suffolk Wildlife Trust 1995
Beardall, C.H. Dryden, R.C.& Holzer,T.J. *The Suffolk Estuaries*, SWT Report, Segment 1988
Butcher, David R. *Waveney Valley*, East Anglian Magazine 1975
Chadwick, Lee *In Search of Heathland*, Dennis Dobson 1982
Dymond, D. & Northeast, P. *A History of Suffolk*, Phillimore, Revised 1995
Dymond, D. & Martin, E. Ed. *An Historical Atlas of Suffolk*, Suffolk County Council 1989
Edwards, Russell *The Suffolk Coast*, Terence Dalton 1991
Holmes, M.R.J. *Suffolk Observed*, Ian Henry 1993
Hoskins, W.G. *English Landscapes*, BBC 1979
Jebb, Miles *Suffolk*, Pimlico 1995
Mason, H.J. & McClelland, A. *Background to Breckland*, Providence 1994
Moore, Derek Ed. *Watching Wildlife in Suffolk*, SWT 1994
Page, William *The Victoria History of the County of Suffolk* Vol.II, Dawson 1975
Rackham, Oliver *The History of the Countryside*, Weidenfeld & Nicholson 1995 edn.
Rackham, Oliver *Trees and Woodland in the British Landscape*, Revised edn, 1993
Rhodes, Celia *Tarpan: The Polish Ponies of Redgrave and Lopham Fen*, SWT 1996
Scarfe, Norman, *The Suffolk Landscape*, Hodder & Stoughton 1972. Revised edn. Alastair Press 1987
Scarfe, Norman *The Suffolk Guide*, 4th edn, Alastair Press 1988
Seeds of Change; A Future for Wildlife and Farming in Suffolk, SWT 1996
Suffolk Womens Institute, *Suffolk Village Book*, Countryside Books & SFWI 1991
Tennyson, Julian *Suffolk Scene*, Blackie 1939. Alastair Press
Warner, Peter *Greens, Commons and Clayland Colonization*, Leicester University Press 1987
Williamson, Tom, Parish Boundaries and early fields. *Journal of Historical Geography* 12 (1986) 249–267

USEFUL ADDRESSES

Suffolk Wildlife Trust
Brooke House
The Green
Ashbocking
Ipswich
Suffolk IP6 9JY

Tel. 01473–890089

English Nature
Norman Tower
1–2 Crown Street
Bury St Edmunds
Suffolk IP33 1QX

Tel. 01284–762218

Forest Enterprise
Tangham
Woodbridge
Suffolk IP12 3NF

Tel. 01394–450214

Woodland Trust
Autumn Park
Dysart Road
Grantham
Lincs. NG31 6LL

Tel. 01476–74297

National Trust
Blickling Hall
Blickling
Norfolk
NR11 6NF

Tel. 01263-733471

Suffolk Coast & Heaths Project
County Highways Department
Dock Lane
Melton
Suffolk
IP12 1PE

Tel. 01394–348948